American Perversity

Sex, Politics and Religion

By

William Bradford Borden

This book is a work of non-fiction. Names and places have been changed to protect the privacy of all individuals. The events and situations are true.

© 2004 by William Bradford Borden. All rights reserved.

No part of this book may be reproduced, stored in a retrieval system, or transmitted by any means, electronic, mechanical, photocopying, recording, or otherwise, without written permission from the author.

ISBN: 1-4140-3294-3 (Paperback)
ISBN: 1-4140-3293-5 (Dust Jacket)

This book is printed on acid free paper.

1stBooks - rev. 03/03/04

**For my mother—
May she one day be proud for bringing me into this world.**

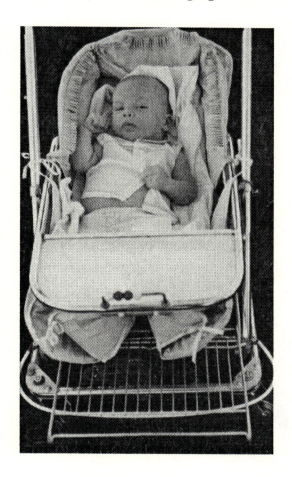

iv

Table Of Contents

Introduction... vii

SEXSTUN I: SEX 1
Chapter 1: The Easter Bunny.. 3
Chapter 2: Muchas Gracias.. 17
Chapter 3: Affirmative Action 29

SEXSOME II: POLITICS 43
Chapter 4: Earth Mother.. 45
Chapter 5: Black Magic 61
Chapter 6: Horticulture 77
Chapter 7: Go For Broke.. 95

SEXSHUN III: RELIGION 115
Chapter 8: Far From Mary 117
Chapter 9: Rise Again 131
Chapter 10: America 151

Epilogue 165
Acknowledgements 169
About the Author.. 175

v

vi

Introduction

What are the three things that one should not discuss in public to avoid confrontation? What are the three things that people hold so personal that they are willing to kill and die for them? If you answered sex, politics and religion, you're right.

Sex, politics and religion, although highly controversial are also the three most personal and, hence, most interesting topics to discuss. Discussions of these topics scare many people. Does it scare you, bother you or annoy you? Do you search within?

My intention with this book is to employ the Socratic dialogue that, in essence, says that the questions we ask of others and ourselves are ultimately more important than the answers. My goal is to continually question things, peel away the layers and tear down the walls. I also hope to question some of your realities.

This book was a labor of love, so I hope you will not take offense at its content. Yes, much that is written you may not agree with—some that I have written I don't agree with—but what kind of world would it be if we all agreed? Maybe better, and yet...

And yet I am angered, saddened and disappointed that so many of us in this most majestic of countries, have become so complacent, so subdued, so reticent, that the very questioning, searching and exploring for truth has been relegated to sheepish acquiescence to an almost surreal subjugation by the powers that be...

May we all find our own power. May we discover again the god, the magic and the wonder that lie within. May we do what is right and make the world a better place.

William Bradford Borden

19 September 2003

Lady Lake, Ansel Adams Wilderness

Central Sierra, California

One more stop before we begin our journey. I present a letter from a former student who wrote it in the front of the journal she gave me as a present. That journal was the first of four that I wrote in by hand to write this book. The beautiful brown leather journal was a gift of love that inspired me greatly. These are her words.

Mr. Borden,   August 24, 2001

There are times when I need a certain indescribable element present in my life. It is a fine gift when I find that element at the time in a person. Although I do not necessarily agree completely with everything that person says or does, I see many things in them that I admire or respect, as these people are intelligent and inspirational. These people are unique; I know that I will never meet another quite like them.

Thank you for being one of these people to me.

Today you asked me jokingly, "What is the secret to happiness?" Now that I think about it, I know that it cuts down to one thing: balance. May your "elements" always be fulfilled and your life full of stories worth writing.

Love,

Shirley Pakdaman

SEXSTUN I: SEX

2

1

The Easter Bunny

When I was about 12 years old, I found about 300 Canadian dollars, wrapped in a rubber band on the ground in an airport. My parents had me turn in the money, and after no one claimed it the money was mailed to me a couple of months later. I spent the money on stocks, and the stocks I bought were Ramada Inn, Pioneer Hi-Bred and Playboy.

I remember seeing my first *Playboy* at around that same age and I was immediately hooked by the glossy centerfolds. Who were these women, these girls, these divas who attracted 12-year-old boys? Were these the same women who would instill in me a Peter Pan Complex and a desire to always be a boy and play? Certainly *Playboy* was at the forefront of the sexual revolution and I came into the world in 1961 when the explosion of sex, drugs and rock-and-roll was about to scintillate, titillate and satiate the world. The revolution had begun and I was one of the foot soldiers. I was ready to fight, my weapon was constantly in hand and I was constantly practicing, firing it off at paper targets that most certainly did not look like the enemy—she did, however look foreign.

The leader of this *Playboy* army was Hugh Hefner. "I never intended to be a revolutionary," he said. "My intention was to create a magazine that included sex in it. That turned out to be a revolutionary idea." Hefner, joined the U.S. Army in 1944 after finishing high school, and served as an infantry clerk, where he drew cartoons for Army newspapers. *Playboy,* in fact, is famous for its

3

William Bradford Borden

cartoons and probably is a result of Hefner's interest in the visual medium of cartoons and photography.

He was born on April 9, 1926, in Chicago, and like other "generals" he was extremely bright. Although he was just an average student, he did possess a genius IQ and started developing drawing techniques and writing for the school newspaper that he started. He also served as president of the student council.

I wonder what it would have been like to go to school with Hefner in those years right before WWII. I remember how awkward my high school years were and I remember the first time I had sex, real sex, the whole thing, the complete act, and the consummation. I remember the act so vividly, as I'm sure most people do, and I also clearly remember the aftermath and my behavior and demeanor with the young lady who started me on my way to becoming a playboy.

In 1975, I was a gangly freshman at a New Jersey high school where many of the student's parents commuted to New York City. The central Jersey school, about 45 minutes from "the city," was extremely diverse, with a strong mix of Irish, Italians, Puerto Ricans, Blacks, Jews and Norwegians. Having Norwegian blood (my mother was born on a ship to a Norwegian mother) I think snow skiing was in my blood. So I joined the ski club, where every Friday afternoon during the winter a bus would depart from the school and we would head for Great Gorge, Vernon Valley.

Those times were great times, trying times and definitely high times. On one trip, the eventful one, I hooked up with the sister of one of my friends and we started to take some runs together. She had a very attractive face and could best be described as full-bodied-lass. As we rode up the lifts we started drinking the miniature bottles of liquor I had brought. This was a common practice and I remember once one kid taking a hard fall and breaking a brandy bottle on his ass. He required stitches, but at least he was anaesthetized and cleansed with alcohol.

So, as this nubile maiden and I continued to drink, we started to touch and rub and knead, and our needs became intense and on each lift ride up we progressed with our exploration, probing forbidden zones, seeking carnal knowledge, lusting for one another. We also

American Perversity
Sex, Politics and Religion

smoked a couple of joints and by that time we were feeling very horny.

It was customary to meet back at the buses at around 10:30 p.m., so we only had time for about one more run. We got off the lift and the lights provided us with ambience and led us at the top of the New Jersey mountain into the trees on that frigid night. When we found a secluded place, we laid down our jackets and took off our skis but left on our bulky boots. Both of us were wearing jeans, and as we lay down I laid her back and awkwardly helped her pull her jeans down to her boots. So here I was; here we were, the moment of truth, the moment of connection, of entry, of change, of transformation—the moment that *Playboy* had prepared me for, the moment the target practice had primed me for.

The entry wasn't easy because of the clumsiness and bulkiness of the boots and jeans, but it was consummated and completed. There were no orgasms or eruptions on either of our parts. I think the fluids would have frozen. And so that moment is frozen in time, but there is more, another moment in a deeper freeze of memory that retains a stiffness all its own. Returning to the bus, I walked down the aisle of the chartered bus. Midway down on the right hand aisle, she had saved the window seat for me. I glanced at the seat and I walked right to the back of the bus where I found my buddies. That moment, that look, that movement, is forever frozen in my mind.

There was no braggadocio, no re-telling the story; instead, there was a sense of guilt, a sense of embarrassment, and a sense of change. Change, they say, is inevitable, and so I was on the hunt for more. I loved the wildlife and was constantly tracking a variety of animals, from beaver and pussy, to ass and bunny. I had become the consummate rabbit; I had become a private in General Hefner's Playboy Army. I was ready to take orders, ready to take chances and ready for the revolution. How quickly I would begin to rise through the ranks.

My first true love, first crush, first woman of my dreams was a stunning blonde Norwegian. We met in seventh grade and I was immediately drawn to her sensuality, her style and smile. Hefner's first love, or rather the siren/muse that launched his offensive was another blonde; her name was Marilyn. In 1953, eight years before

William Bradford Borden

my birth and 50 years from when I pen these thoughts, Hefner issued his first *Playboy* magazine featuring the famous calendar shot of Marilyn Monroe. He had produced this magazine at his dining table in his South Side apartment and there was no cover date because he wasn't sure if he could produce another. How surprised he must have been when the first issue sold more than 50,000 copies—cluster bombs, if you will, in the propaganda war of the beginning of the sexual revolution.

My blonde Norwegian bombshell often made it difficult to stand in our eighth grade class, because my artillery piece was constantly coming to attention. Maybe that and my own Scandinavian connection made me fall in love not only with her, but also with the Beatles and, in particular, a song called "Norwegian Wood." I could definitely relate to Norwegian wood! Would it have mattered if I had been born 10 years before, in 1951? Certainly, and yet, I remember much of the '60s. Although I wasn't old enough to be a real warrior in Vietnam, or a true civil rights protester, or a verified hippie, I still vividly remember the mood and the feel of the '60s. I have often thought that I would have liked to live on a commune with lots of free love and kinship.

My high school experience wasn't nearly as successful as Hefner's. In the middle of my senior year, sick and tired of the bullshit I left school to live on the streets and at the downtown YMCA in Phoenix, where I would be beaten nearly to death by two vicious black teens. In 1979, when my fellow New Jersey seniors were going to the prom, I saw the Village People doing a promo shoot for their song "YMCA."

I didn't know at the time that some of the Village People were rip-roaring homosexuals; but it didn't really matter. At that time I was so lost. I also didn't know that for many the YMCA was a Mecca for homosexuals. I have never had a homosexual experience, nor been interested in one, for I worship and adore women; but I've always had a strong affinity toward many homosexuals, including some of my favorite professors.

I'm not sure what Hefner's views are on homosexuality, but I'm sure—like a strong percentage of men—he is an advocate of bisexuality in women. I find that rather erotic myself. I think, if I

American Perversity
Sex, Politics and Religion

were a parent, I would have less of a problem with a daughter being bisexual than a son, and I think bisexuality in women is in some ways more natural than it is in men.

In high school I was with all of three women, each all of one time: one on the ski slopes; one up against a wall at a party; and one in the backyard, on my back with a luscious pixie on top. After returning briefly for graduation (I had enough credits to graduate), I was back out to Arizona, to Arizona State where I played soccer, drank like a fish, got high and tried desperately to find myself.

To find oneself, I have learned, is not always, or even often, fruitful under the influence of sex, drugs and rock-and-roll. It is, however, this search for self, often more exploratory and self-actualizing. Even as I reflect on those ideas, I'm not sure if I quite agree. What I do agree upon is that through sex, drugs and rock-and-roll (and I don't want to kill the term) you are often led on some special trips and journeys you might not regularly take.

So the journeys led me to some different paths, through some different decisions to some different destinations. In my senior year at Arizona State I had a marginal 2.0 G.P.A. and I was trying to get my act together by pursuing a career as an Army officer. The summer before I had spent six weeks at Fort Knox in Army officer training, courtesy of the Reserve Officer Training Corps (ROTC), but I didn't like the Army at that point. So in my senior year I dropped out of Arizona State and joined the Marine Corps and continued in pursuit of conquests, both foreign and domestic.

My first two years were spent in El Toro, Calif., with weekends often at Laguna Beach. I had visited California as a child, but it was with a sense of wonder and amazement that I had returned to the Golden State. The place where so much of the way the country and hence the world is influenced by the culture and dreams of the people. The year was 1984, the Olympics came to Los Angeles, Randy Newman sang about loving it, and I fell in love with the music of The Doors.

Many doors opened for me and a great opportunity came when I was given orders to Iwakuni, Japan, just south of Hiroshima, to the Third Marine Air Wing. There is a saying in the Corps, "Swing with

7

William Bradford Borden

the wing," and that is exactly what I did, in that being a part of the air wing was not only an honor but also a privilege.

In 1985 the dollar to the yen was extremely strong and I was a relatively affluent lance corporal. The first month "in country" I went out with corporals Davila and Kimball and we stopped in at a little restaurant called the Taco House. I always wash my hands before eating, and as I headed toward the bathroom, at the end of the taco bar sat a gorgeous Japanese girl with friends in tow.

With my very limited Japanese, I asked, "O gen ki deska bijin?" which translates, "How are you doing pretty girl?" "Fine," she responded in perfect English and a chance meeting with the woman who would become my personal geisha girl began. Miyuki had been an exchange student in California during high school and spoke fluent English. She had acquired a love of Mexican food and tacos, so that is how it all began. Life is full of chance meetings. It is so often in that fraction of a moment that a connection is bound with one who ultimately affects our lives more than we can imagine.

Japan, largely because of Miyuki, was a terrific experience. From a playboy point of view, the Love Hotels, which are ever present in Japan, were a wonderful training ground for my Asian invasion. The Japanese are a people that, unlike Americans where the individual and independence are so prized, believe that the society, the whole, the culture itself, takes precedence over the people that make up that society.

Japan is a society that often wears a mask, and so the sexuality and the nuances of what is being conveyed is often difficult to ascertain. It is a society, like many societies, where the men are seemingly in power, but where the women wield tremendous influence and control. I am reminded of the story of the young girl who sees the boy next door urinating and is transfixed seeing his instrument for the first time. She runs into the house to her mother, crying and complaining that she doesn't have one of those, one of those man things, the other head; and her mother calms her and tells her that with one of what she has, she can have as many of those as she wants.

Before I leave Japan, I must go into detail about the Love Hotels. Because housing in Japan is so critical and young people often live at

American Perversity
Sex, Politics and Religion

home until marriage, they need a place to go for sex. These hotels, with their gaudy, Las Vegas-like fluorescent lights usually have different theme rooms. You drive in, much like a drive-in fast food place and look at pictures of what the rooms look like. They range anywhere from traditional Samurai-style rooms, to Wild West, to ultra-modern, 21st century rooms; all in the epicenter of Hiroshima, location, location, location. If the light for the desired room were on, you would pull into the respective parking space and walk upstairs directly to the room.

There were condoms, coffee, porn movies, deep bathtubs. All in a spotless, sanitary and serene space that was most conducive to sexual pleasure. It was possible even to take the room for three hours and you would pay via a vacuum tube (never actually meeting the receptionist), where you insert the money and then receive change and receipt. It was a terrific concept.

While in Japan, I had the opportunity to go to Korea twice on operations and it was there I enjoyed Korean-style sexual hospitality. This is made even more sensual and erotic by the futons that are placed on the floors, which are heated by charcoal that burns beneath. I found it strange that many of the same Marines whom I would see at a church service or on the flight line with their families would, a week or so later in Korea, be at the bar with some Asian goddess, and at the next moment, be exiting stage right for some personal entertainment.

Personal entertainment is also, or rather was before the U.S. pulled out, an integral part of the Philippine economy. Before I had even arrived in the Philippines (our squadron deployed for the 1985 Marcos-Aquino election) I had heard about the LBFM's, the "Little Brown Fucking Machines," and I was amazed at the decadence and the degree that women, young women, very young women at that, would do things for money. This is not a new concept. What concepts are new anyway, and, for that matter, who knew?

Now a blonde socialite enters the Starbucks: khaki skirt, beige top, hot legs and body, debutante, Huntington Gardens, Pasadena type, probably transplanted to Bel Air—an actress perhaps—bent on sexual perversion I imagine, intelligent and social. I wonder when her birthday is, what her sign is, and I wonder if she tells the truth. I

William Bradford Borden

imagine she might play truth or dare, and it is a daring endeavor, the games, full of sexual innuendo, of play, wanting to get laid.

It is now, about twenty minutes later, and blonde socialite corrected me and said that Pasadena is Newport; and I read her the above, and she said I got it about right; how could I get it wrong, a lady in waiting, waiting to get laid. "Let me give you my number," she suggests. Her number will be called, she will be served, customer service, handling the products, wrapping her up in ribbons and bows, a pretty pink one at the fork of her soul, and the present is untied and opened and it is an elegant vase with lovely trim and it is already moist, ready for the long stem to touch her bottom, and the moisture erupts as the flowers are pollinated. She exits the bathroom and I come back to the moment.

I wonder if the White House bathrooms have bidets. I think it's absurd that we don't use bidets more in America. Many Americans have never even seen a bidet. The Italians and French use bidets and their women are known for their freshness, their allure, and their culinary delights. I wonder if Bridget Bardot's bidet is used every day. Maybe, to bring the wonderful French back into favor, and honor them, we could have a National Bidet Day. The French know the value of health, of wine, of fine dishes—especially the fresh fish, cleansed and prepared properly, ready to be savored, consumed and devoured.

I think it's a wonderful idea, perhaps my first production, a training video, with my production company BOMWISH. Maybe, I'll have one of Bush's biggest supporters, the ballsy Michael Moore, the vocal Academy Award winner for the amazing *Bowling for Columbine* and the author of the must read *Stupid White Men*, direct. Charlton Heston could handle the bidet, Dick Clark could narrate and Bridget Bardot could play herself. Maybe Charlton could spread the waters again and help Dick to get Bridget to open up. The production could be called *Bridget Bardot's Bidet*. Sure, the whole thing could get a bit hairy; hairy for the French is Moore, and Moore is also hairy for Bush.

Sex, like religion and politics, often has an addictive quality and so, in 1986, the last year in Japan, I "found Jesus." I had been raised in the Episcopal Church, the high church, country club/society

American Perversity
Sex, Politics and Religion

church, the church of many U.S. Presidents, and now, I had found Jesus. After two years of Jesus, and much of this I will relate later (and I hope you stick around for later because it gets much better; this is a parenthetical note that I am inserting months after penning this first chapter and I realize how stilted and contrived much of the beginning is and how much smoother it all begins to flow as I get into the groove.)

Yes, after two years of celibacy, self-righteousness and Jesus, I met Sinead (not her real name), who was 18 to my 27, with beautiful skin, fine blonde hair, shapely hips and firm "B" breasts. She was a perfect 5'9" wonder who I looked at the first week the Women Studies class met, talked with the second and moved in with the third. We lived together for almost a year and she inspired me with her humor, intelligence and laughter. She also taught me about pain, trust and companionship. We broke up on my birthday with her throwing my presents at me and me throwing away an angel.

During my second year of graduate school (I had stayed on at the University of North Carolina at Charlotte to pursue a Master in English) another angel came, in the form of death, to take away my real god, my father—not in heaven, but in New Jersey. A couple of weeks before his massive heart attack at 65, I told him that I wanted to be an actor. He said then that if I wanted to act, just act, just do it. It was years before Nike would tell us the same thing.

At my dad's funeral, Sergio, who had worked with my dad for more than 20 years, suggested I go to Italy, learn Italian, and start doing the work my dad had established with an Italian friend, importing wine, pasta and olive oil. I went to Rome over spring break, picked up *Wanted in Rome*, a newspaper for ex-patriots, and saw an advertisement that caught my eye and changed my life.

The ad was looking for an actor to play the role of a teacher in an English language video entitled, *UK, US, You Too*. I met with the producer, Elisabetta, who had met with more than 40 candidates, and was offered the job, which would start shooting in late August; so, I could wrap up my affairs and finish my degree. She asked me how much I would want for the three-month shoot, and using the best line I've ever used in business, I asked what she was offering, and when she gave me a number that was three times more than what I had in

William Bradford Borden

mind, I kept the straightest face possible, leaned forward and agreed that I thought I could do it for that sum—and so my Italian training, another two-year mission, this time as a civilian, was about to begin.

I took Elisabetta up on her offer to join the party on Stromboli, a live volcano off the coast of Sicily, in the Aeolian Islands. There were no cars on the Ginostra side and donkeys transported all goods. The island was nude in most places and I loved lounging around on the huge boulders and swimming al fresco in the beautiful Mediterranean.

The Italians, like the French, are some of the most sensual people I've ever met in all my world travels...

I must digress and return to Charlotte for a moment to an Italian-American girl named Aretha (not her real name) whom I met at a beauty school where I went for cheap haircuts. I ended up falling in love with this Leo goddess, after Sinead, and then left her behind and left for Italy. I should have taken her with me, but I didn't because she wasn't "educated" and I thought she'd always just be a stylist. I didn't realize all the potential and the power that this young 20-year-old would muster, and open several successive and successful salons, which would become the fixture of Charlotte, N.C., which is rapidly becoming a fixture in U.S. banking. She was money in the bank and I was a fool parted.

Continually restless, I was constantly seeking new venues, new conquests, and new territory. In real estate the three most important concepts are location, location and location; so it has become with me in regards to sex—location, location, location, as opposed to position, position, position. Although, an argument might be made that the two are rather synonymous. Sure, I've perused the *Kama Sutra*, but ultimately there is only a handful of positions that I really enjoy and, for that matter, a handful of locations.

In Italy, I had the opportunity to work as an actor for more than two years and even starred as the American writer Eugene Carter in the Italian Film, *Una Casa Sotto il Cielo* (*A House Under the Sky*) which won several awards at film festivals. I also had the opportunity to work with Nick Nolte, F. Murray Abraham and Ben Cross. In my second year in Rome, I moved in with three girls—two Italian sisters and a German girl, Julia. On the top floor of that building lived the

American Perversity
Sex, Politics and Religion

world-famous pornographer, Alberto Ferro, aka Lasse Braun, who had made his first million by the age of 30 in the late '60s.

Alberto had been born into a wealthy Italian family and his father had been part of Mussolini's cabinet. In fact, Alberto's older brother, who would later become a prominent judge, was held in the arms of Hitler as a baby. Alberto himself was a lawyer but decided he wanted to be part of the sexual revolution, and so he pursued a career that would make him one of the true leaders of the fight. His film *Sensations,* hardcore porn, shot on 35mm would become the hit of the Cannes Film Festival and rocket him to the top.

In my second year in Rome I began working for Alberto, who was at that time focusing on erotic thrillers. I even wrote a script for him called *Separate Bedrooms,* which I took great pride in writing, but we never produced. I always found Alberto honest, intelligent and engaging, and he in essence became a mentor who would follow me back to Los Angeles where we would open an office at Raleigh Studios and come so close to a big-time deal, which in essence was there, but then it wasn't... So Alberto moved into my house, his son would follow, and we tried to get several projects off the ground, but eventually Alberto returned to pornography, of which I was not against, but was also not necessarily interested in being involved in. What was anticipated as a three-month visit turned into a three-year stay and it was during that time that I returned to teaching.

When a rowdy group of students asked me what I had been doing in Italy, I said I had been acting, and this cocky kid said, "Yeah, you were a porn star." Although he was wrong, he didn't know how close he was to the reality, and so a legend was born that would grow to the point where people swore they saw me in films and that I was the "pool man." I almost started to believe it myself, and at the high school where I taught it even got to the point where the principal asked my boss, the wonderful Ms. B.G. if she knew that Mr. Borden was a porn star, and B.G. slyly replied that was the reason she hired me.

I will take a break—promenade, like a horse, up and down the boulevard—and remember my lovely Nectarine, who, when I entered her, thick and deep, my stallion to her mare, and Nectarine, the name I gave her after I tasted her and I said it was the nectar of the gods, and

William Bradford Borden

it was, fruity and juicy, healthy, like she, and I mounted her, first like a missionary, as I first tasted her lower, peach-fuzzed lips, and then slobbered my lips onto her mouth, re-circulating her flowing juices, and I squeezed the juices out of her, and the cycle was completed and I made my pronouncements, but she needed no conversion. She was a willing follower as she submitted to my sermon, on the mount, and she recited a poem of love she had remembered, and the memory is now, and I would love to go riding with my Nectarine again, with blanket and without, bareback, and the juices would be shared, inside and out, and eggs are also counted, and the weekend is a nice time to have eggs, to share in the moment and break the fast…

I wonder what they have for breakfast at the Playboy Mansion. I think I'd like to have my own playboy pad, complete with dance studio, library, gym, infinity pool, breathtaking gardens, and tennis court. Maybe up on Mullholland, looking out over L.A. where I could race my car on the weekends. But now back to reality or perceptions thereof…

A delusional, homeless woman, pushing 60 or 70, dirty, easily 100 pounds overweight, white, unkempt hair—repelling—enters. She carries on a conversation, on a cellular that is almost assuredly not functioning, but her delusions are, and her conversation, with fantasy, is a harsh reality, and yet she is communicating to the public. There is still radiance, an aura, a fading star, and she continues her dialogue, starting to believe the conversation herself.

"Fucking dim, no one likes him." She is the only woman in this section, and one white-haired man has his fingers in his ears, and she is irritating, yet fascinating. Now something about picking up a dead son somewhere, "He couldn't win if you gave him $50," maybe 50 is a good amount to bet and she continues, "You're putting a Don Juan next to a Casanova." You don't even have to pay this gusher for dialogue, just listen and observe, and I look to my right, out the window, by the door, and I see the black handle of the broom she uses like a walking stick to promenade, and then "Shit no, I'd kill my husband…if I were that type of person."

I wonder about marriage, about the recent revelations about JFK, Jr.'s troubled marriage (and seniors as well for that matter) and the catastrophic divorce rate. I am putting the finishing touches on this

American Perversity
Sex, Politics and Religion

chapter and typing directly into my laptop. I realize I prefer writing by hand and then transcribing, which is certainly more work, but to me has a greater feel of artistry, of soul and self, instead of this connection with machine.

Just a thought: I think I should like to have a long engagement, perhaps seven years, and if there is no itching, then perhaps get married. I figure, if I never get married, then I'll never get divorced and I remember a friend (who was happily married) asking if I would get on a plane if I knew it had a 50 percent chance of crashing. And so I think, in many respects it takes more commitment to live with someone than to be married. Sure you can do both, but...

On the cover of the June 30, 2003, *Newsweek* is a picture of a couple in bed, he with his glasses on the bridge of his nose, leaned up against the headboard with laptop on lap and she, also up against headboard, spoon in right hand, ice cream in left, watching television. And in the middle of the cover, in white, across their genitals, the proclamation "No Sex, Please, We're Married," and then under that, a question, "Are Stress, Kids and Work Killing Romance?" And maybe the question is rhetorical, but I would answer yes, and the fact Americans are working themselves to death, and for what purpose as the average American takes 10 days of vacation while their British counterparts double that and our elected officials, off at the ranch, on the trail, or in recess probably quadruple that, and yet marriage is continually encouraged and praised with tax incentives and yet, what are the alternatives?

A week later, in the July 7, 2003, *Newsweek*, there is a cover article with two very attractive lesbians "Partners Lauren Leslie and Elisabeth Noel Jones," and they look happy, satisfied, and gay (apparently there was a sister cover that was released at the same time with two handsome homosexuals), and the question here is, "Is Gay Marriage Next?" And to that I answer or rather question, "Is marriage at all next?" I don't think I will even attempt to answer these questions but I would suggest that Hefner and his band of beauties certainly appear a lot happier and healthier than the average bear, and yet can we bear to bare our souls, to strip ourselves and expose our own realities or are we all just a bit delusional as the crazy woman continues—but wait—maybe she's not homeless after all.

William Bradford Borden

Speaking into her cellular (and everyone hears her now, except perhaps the imaginary friend on the "other line") she powerfully proclaims, "That's my mansion...don't you have any dignity about you?" and then, and I feel like I'm getting to know her better, "I'm particular, Honey, you need to ask me," and now she says, "Believe it or not..." and I want to answer "No! I don't believe you!" But go on, it's still a good story, and in many respects that is what our lives are: stories, full of pages, chapters and volumes.

2
Muchas Gracias

Jennifer Lopez could have been a Playboy bunny, for few women are blessed with such a shapely shape—a shape for sex, for movement, for grandeur. Therefore, I pay tribute to a woman who has surpassed the likes of Don Juan and Valentino and ascended the crown and taken the title of the preeminent Latin lover. This Puerto Rican American, Bronx N.Y.-born, Latina goddess, this woman, now known as J. Lo, can sing, and dance, and act with such brilliance, to make her one of the most viable triple threats in Hollywood. The fact that J. Lo has taken over as the symbol of Latin love is tremendously ironic, as seemingly the force of machismo has abdicated its power. This power, lost to this Leo diva, is an extremely important cultural phenomenon as the Latin people surpass blacks as the largest minority in America. She is certainly on the cutting edge of change.

Growing up outside of New York, I had a lot of contact with Puerto Ricans. I remember in eighth grade, a Puerto Rican kid named Ricky, who looked twenty-something, pulling out chains in a hallway brawl with a hulking white kid named Bruce, who'd probably started shaving when he was in fourth grade. I also remember going to our church in New Brunswick and hearing my father speak excellent Spanish (he spent two years in Mexico City after WWII and graduated from Mexico City College) to a group of potential Puerto Rican Boy Scouts who had just been rumbling. It reminded me, or

17

William Bradford Borden

later would trigger that reaction of fascination, to my experiences with theatre and in particular *West Side Story*.

The thought of these Puerto Ricans as Boy Scouts, 30 or so years later seems strange in that Hispanic males always seem so grown-up, so mature, and so macho, that the idea of scouting seems odd. So does my commentary, I realize, because later, when I was in the Marines, I came to find many Hispanics in the military, wearing uniforms and enjoying being part of an organized, disciplined and highly formidable fighting force. I wonder if J. Lo has entertained the troops, because entertaining she most certainly is. In many respects she is the consummate pin-up and she earned the nickname "la guitara" as a young girl because of her shapely shape. To keep her in shape were her father, a computer specialist, and her mother, a schoolteacher. She also has two sisters, Maria and Linda, and as I understand it, she is often attended by a massive entourage to satisfy her massive…

In Living Color was one of J. Lo's first breaks, but what about other Latinos and theirs? I am caught in the moment of a moment ago when a Hispanic man, probably around my age but looking older, crossed the street after entering and then exiting Studio City Camera Exchange, where, apparently, he didn't sell any of the strawberries he held and still holds and may always hold. And so I am held with that image as the light changes, and it relates to another of my theories. The theory relates to nature and I call it the "Strawberry Theory," and I thank the Hispanic man, who was more Indian than Spanish for being green-lighted, perhaps without a green card, at the moment he was.

I will attempt to connect the Strawberry with both coasts and with two high schools 20 years apart. In 1979, while living at the YMCA I helped save an elderly Hispanic man whose face had been stomped as he lay sleeping on a doorstep across the city street. Pulling the arm off a beat-up old chair, I ran from the T.V. room where I had been watching Larry Bird and the NCAA Basketball Tournament. With my makeshift weapon in hand I confronted—along with another person of the village, a middle-aged Hispanic man—a young black teen on a bicycle who reached for something shiny in his belt and then rode off as a crowd gathered.

American Perversity
Sex, Politics and Religion

The summer before my time in Phoenix, in the year between my junior and senior year of high school, I had gone to Monterrey, Mexico, to study Spanish, play soccer and stay with an elite Mexican family, which had befriended my father decades before. I learned about Spanish gatherings and a lot about Mexican culture, which is different from the Puerto Rican but also alike in so many ways. I learned about gatherings.

After my four-month hiatus to Phoenix, I returned back to New Jersey and was there in time for lots of the graduation parties. Because the drinking age was then 18, many of the parties were stocked with kegs and most of us drank huge quantities of beer. At one of the graduation parties, there were probably well over 200 people and ample kegs. I was in the back, sitting with my first love, knee to knee, discussing music, life, people, and then someone came to the back and said there were a bunch of Puerto Ricans in front and they were causing trouble. So I went out, and we confronted the guys, whom I didn't know.

It was 1979 and Bruce Lee and karate movies were big. One of the Puerto Ricans pulled out a set of nun chucks (which are bamboo polls attached with a chain in the middle; one is held, the other's used to strike), and because I was saying to them in the Spanish I had so impressively learned, "chinga tu madre," or "fuck your mother," this one young guy swung his weapon at me. I blocked with my arm, which was immediately swollen and piercing with pain, and so I quickly took him down and proceeded to smash his face into the street and leave him there, alive but in need of serious dental work. I can, I realize, be so, so animal-like to such a degree that the rage and fury often scare the hell out of me.

It has been said that there are two ways to build the tallest building in a city. One is to tear down all buildings taller than yours, which is what most of us seem to do, and the other is to build your building taller than all the rest. The latter usually takes more effort and skill but is ultimately much more rewarding. I have also come to realize that I'd rather build up than tear down.

America is not the United States, in certain or uncertain geographic or topographic terms. Much of the Latin world is America, and we in America seem to think that we are American.

William Bradford Borden

The name America comes from an Italian explorer, Vespucci, but there are North, Central, and South America, along with the United States of… and I realize I still don't have a solid transition.

Maybe the transition itself is in the form of maps and the world, and so I move 20 years, from 1979 to 1999, from a New Jersey high school to a Los Angeles one, from the role of student to the role of teacher. I hated most of high school when I was there…

But this is so contrived. I'm starting another day in L.A., where I listen to a group of women, three generations, discussing cars, laughing, and enjoying the California sun. A beautiful black kid, pushed by a mocha-colored, Rasta man, his dreads flowing and one of the women, kind of country-type, Dixie Chick, and she says to the black man that the stroller looks like a "luxury ride," and they laugh and get back to talking about cars and California and actors—in particular some actor who's apparently a "dumb fuck."

Then a kid, definitely an affluent kid, and probably a kid of '60s parents, walks past into the Starbucks, clad in camouflage pants. Now, I overhear the youngest of the 'chicks,' maybe 16, with a clear, precise, Valley girl voice explain her views, or at least a commentator's view, of Gulf War II and I am reminded of another day in L.A., and also that I missed John's protest speech.

John, from South Central L.A., called me the other day to see how I was doing. John has a coolness that enables coolness. Coolness seems like one of those hereditary and environment type things. It's a quality that many Latino men have from their seemingly much more macho upbringing. And isn't that really, in essence, what macho means, "much more," and there is much more I need to share, to put down to just a few of the Latino people who have so profoundly impacted my life.

In the L.A. high school, where John was the student and I was the teacher, there were some assumed perception of me as a "gringo." The perceptions it seemed, were sometimes those of "look at what you, you white Europeans did to the Indians and to the slaves," and my retort was to sometimes question their knowledge, heredity and understanding of who they are and where they're from. In fact many, if not in a majority of Latinos, owe their identity to European white men of more southern clime. Europeans, yes, but not white Anglo-

20

American Perversity
Sex, Politics and Religion

Saxon Protestants. No, their identity came from another part of Europe, a place of inquisitive religious influence and oppressive conquest. These men spoke Spanish.

When John called me he was so polite, so excited, such the gentlemen, and I had told him I had moved on to teach college and he thought that was cool, real cool, super-cool. And when I asked him what he was doing and I didn't—because that is what I do quite often—give him a chance to answer, I instead answered for him that he had joined the military and he said, "Nah, Mr. Borden, I'm not in the military. I'm in college and I'm going to teach, just like you. And by the way I'm speaking at Pershing Square Friday." But I missed the speech he was chosen for to speak out in opposition to the war, because I was teaching Shakespeare, Richard III, yes, "A horse, a horse, my kingdom for a horse." How utterly profound—maybe a kid from South Central knows a little about terrorism, oppression and tribal warfare. Who knew? I think maybe John, and I'm also sure that in his own ways John supports the troops and supports America and supports giving peace a chance and I'm drawn to remember one of the reasons I left teaching high school in L.A.

I never got a yearbook my senior year because I was gone for the last half of the school year—the Phoenix had risen. Twenty-one years later, in 2000, I got a yearbook, and in a way I was finally graduating and the students signed the book as such. John wrote the following:

Borden

To the greatest English teacher in my point of view, I would like to take this time to thank you for letting me expand the writing skill I thought I never had, you taught me to understand novels, you taught me to read faster and to enjoy peace and quiet. I guess this will be the last time you hear from your talented surprising English student. As for me I'll be attending NYU and major in drama, thank you for all your support on my struggling acting career, take care of yourself and settle down man, start a damn family.

William Bradford Borden

And then John wrote #32, his football jersey, printed his name and signed beneath. I'm glad John stayed in L.A., although I'm sure someday his West Coast cool will head east.

Before teaching at the high school and before L.A., from 1991-1993, I was living in Rome. When I arrived in Los Angeles in 1993 I opened an office at Raleigh Studios across from Paramount, but due to a financial disaster in a film project gone wrong, I started substitute teaching at one magical middle school where I met a Latina Angel who would change my perspective toward life.

After a half a year subbing frequently and feeling like I was making a difference in young people's lives, I was asked to take over a science class. Science has never been my forte, but in 1995 I met "Angelina," a precocious green-eyed Latina princess with a spark and energy that was highly engaging. One time, when the students were otherwise engaged, she came up to me and innocently, yet with a bit of devil in her magical Mayan/Aztec eyes, leaned forward over the large science counter, and this 15-year-old, the age when similar Latina girls have their Quincenera celebrating their fifteenth birthday—leaned over and asked, "Mr. Borden, what's 69?" And I was amused, taken aback and I smiled back and came back with what I felt was such an appropriate response, "It's the number between 68 and 70." She smiled and went back to her seat.

Trying to wing it, and unfortunately that is the kind of education that many L.A. kids have had—given inexperienced teachers and classes with more people than you would place the same amount of dogs—a generation of kids whose education had literally been robbed. And there I was, trying my hardest and even leading science experiments with a group of Armenian kids who I think at times were intent on blowing up the class.

I remember that same class that Angelina was in. I had a group from UCLA present a program called Education Now and Babies Later (ENABL) and I remember Angelina's leading and provocative questions and how she put the UCLA students on the spot. I also remember a trio of Armenian girls (one of whom would later be my teaching assistant at the high school), and I remember that they weren't comfortable sitting through such a presentation.

American Perversity
Sex, Politics and Religion

The class was rowdy and pushing out-of-control, as middle schools often are with their high octane, explosive hormone condition, and I remember that the three girls were up talking and not in their seats and so I asked one of the kids how to say "sit down and be quiet" in Armenian and he told me and then offered to write it down phonetically. So, I went over to the girls and I started with "Sus mna" which I knew meant, "be quiet" and proceeded to sound out the Armenian phonetics that Sarkis had written, "kunem mamayet." They looked at me puzzled, embarrassed and a bit shocked, and I heard the nasal laughter of the bomber as I was informed by the girls that I was telling them to "sit down" and that I wanted to "fuck their mothers." That was the kind of class Angelina was in.

For the final project assigned to Angelina and her class—and I think I thought of it because I was teaching science, but my background was English, and I thought it would be helpful to them and interesting to me—I had them write about their heredity and environment and how these two aspects of their lives, which Freud felt so important, had made them who they were. I have often kept interesting papers and I came across Angelina's project in January 2000 with a sketched diagram of New York on the front dated June 26, 1995. She starts in that her "Ancestors are all from N.Y. and they all grew up on Long Island. They all spoke English."

"My mom is American and my dad is Hispanic. My dad was born in Mexico. I'm a Catholic. And I did my first communion this year... In April we have this thing where we don't eat meat on Fridays. I don't know why, but I know it's part of my religion."

In her section on environment and heredity, she continues, "All around me right now is gangs, and violence, and drugs. I used to be into all that stuff, but not any more. I stopped doing it all ever since I got caught and got sent to Juvenile Hall. I think about it now and all that stuff wasn't worth it."

She continues in flowing, straight up cursive scribes. "If I don't find new friends this will affect my future. The only things my friends do is cut class and do drugs. If I hang around them I do the same and mess up my future."

As I continue to share Angelina's words, I want you to envision where the young lady who then fifteen would be 22 or 23 today—

23

William Bradford Borden

think of the power of change and transformation. What are young people's goals at that age, those pivotal years between child and adult? I think Angelina had a terrific and realistic goal in mind—a vision, a dream...

"When I grow up I want to work with children. I like kids. I want to help the homeless. Ever since I was about five years old, I felt so bad for homeless people."

I think it's fascinating, and in retrospect I remember introducing to her science class—from my perspective of a teacher with a masters in English with an emphasis in rhetoric—the theories of Freud and how he felt the first five years fundamental in the formation of personality.

Angelina continues: "The biggest issue that I always think about is racist people. I don't understand why people are like this. Everyone is equal. Everybody should be treated exactly the same. That's why we have all this violence everywhere."

Angelina would be moving on and for me that is one of the hardest things about teaching, the constant cycle of hellos and goodbyes. I wonder what Angelina's doing today. I wonder what she does often. I wonder if she's happy. To finish her assignment, Angelina entitled one of her sections—her last section—"Role Model" and she wrote:

"I have no role model. I believe that nobody has to take after no one else, that you are your own person. But I would want to take after my mother because she's a really good person, and one of the perfect mothers in this world." Wow, what a tribute to a mother. Do mothers know how their children feel about them? Do children know how mothers feel about them? Angelina continues:

"I live in a house in North Hollywood. It has four bedrooms and two bathrooms it's really big. The neighborhood is good, only old people around us." I'm happy that Angelina is happy with old people in her neighborhood, her good neighborhood, and she explains, "I live with my mom, stepfather, and three sisters. I'm the second oldest. It's kind of hard being the second oldest because I have to take care of my other sisters and help around the house." I imagine the house is spotless and I can tell that Angelina had put a lot of effort and thought into her project.

American Perversity
Sex, Politics and Religion

"My stepfather's a jerk, I hate him at times, but then again I love him because he raised me since I was 8 months old, so I consider him my real father. It's hard not knowing my father. I feel like I was wanted by him. I've never seen him before and I doubt I will...My mother plays both roles, of the father, and the mother. Without my mother I'd be dead somewhere. I like public schools, but private schools are better, but I'd never go to a private school. I would never go because they are a little too strict, because learning is supposed to be fun at times."

Amen, Angelina, amen. School is supposed to be fun and it was. I would stay on to teach Drama for one period and Special Education before moving on to high school. Angelina would leave that June.

Four years later in January of 2000 I would share the words Angelina had written with my seniors who were about to graduate and I would ask them what they thought she was doing with her life. Many guessed college, some said prison, and a couple knew the answer.

Socrates said that the questions we ask are more important than the answers and when we continually ask, we peel away layers, Angelina was always asking questions.

I found her project in one of my filing cabinets after I decided to sell my house and downsize. I was cleaning out some papers and when I read it I bawled, for I knew some of the answers, but not all, to the question of Angelina.

I wonder what Angelina would have written in my yearbook. In a way, I'm writing in hers. Are you happy, Angelina? Where are you? No, she's not in college, or prison, and no she doesn't have a bunch of kids. No, the answer is that Angelina is dead.

I knew that Angelina had committed suicide a couple of years earlier, since I had heard about it months after. I had now been at the high school for two years and it was almost five since she had submitted her thoughts. And so when they were discovered, I brought them in and read them to my seniors who were writing their autobiographies and I asked them, and I knew my answer, if they thought I should contact the mother and they almost all, most in tears, the tough guys too, agreed I should.

William Bradford Borden

At lunch I shared it with my mentor, Ms. B.G. the magnet coordinator (and a magnet herself) and she said she'd see if she could find a phone number and address. So, right before the sixth and final period, a T.A. returned with Angelina's project and a green Post-It attached, which read:

Mr. Borden,

The last known address and phone number of Angelina was:
Then the address and phone number…
The number of a family friend…
And a note "she passed away 01/21/97."

When I saw the last line I got this mystical, chilling feeling because the date was 1/21/2000. It was the three-year anniversary of the flight of an angel.

Given it was the anniversary of Angelina's death, I waited more than a week to call and I got the stepfather and I told him what I had, and he listened, politely, and I said it said things about him not so nice, like that he was a "jerk and that he drank a lot," but nice things, too, like how he was "like her real father and that he raised her since she was eight months old…"

He stopped me there, and I could hear the restraint and the control, but I also heard the pain and the tears when he told me, "I raised her since she was six months old, six month. She was my girl."

I gave him my number and the mother called later that evening and I told her I could mail it, but I would be honored to bring in to her and she seemed very pleased at that and so I ventured to the "four-bedroom, two-bath North Hollywood house, with mostly old people in the quiet neighborhood."

Angelina's mother, about whom Angelina had written, "I would want to take after my mother because she's a really good person and one of the perfect mothers in the world," that mother, who held in her hands a scrapbook of all things Angelina, a puzzle of a life in pictures and writing. I gave her the final piece and the puzzle was complete.

American Perversity
Sex, Politics and Religion

Angelina's mother presented me with a picture, and on the back was penned, "Angelina 15." It was a snapshot, a snap of a finger of a moment of the life of a Latina girl whose mother sobbed and said "I never knew what my daughter thought of me." Now she did, now she does. Are you smiling Angelina? I hope so. I miss you.

28

3
Affirmative Action

I'm still stuck on this affirmative action thing. I do want to present a reflective, balanced and provocative perspective, but something perplexes me. If "diversity," a euphemism it seems for quotas, is acceptable in academic America, why not athletic America? Asians, it seems, are terribly underrepresented, as are Latinos and Arabs, on the NCAA basketball and football squads. Wouldn't a bit more diversity be interesting and just, or would it be more interesting and just for the best qualified in both arenas to be chosen?

In the musical arena Eminem (whose real name is Marshall Mathers) has been chosen. Chosen by who might be the argument, as arguments can be made for virtually any idea or thought, including my prior paragraph, for which I also struggle with the merits. Eminem was also chosen, and ascended the throne because he was the best qualified, most talented and the best ambassador...

A very heavy, actually obese woman walks into the Starbucks and I am reminded of Eminem's apparent cruelty and misogyny towards all kinds of women. Many of those inflammatory references seem misguided and even hateful, but then he's got a sweet side when he sings to his daughter Haley. That's just a comment. I don't want to whitewash things, but I do want to pay tribute to his power of transformation and connect it, like music connects us to one another, in both a literal and figurative sense.

William Bradford Borden

I would imagine that when Eminem raps about raping his mother he is not being literal, but the figurative alternative is not readily apparent. He continually spouts oedipal spawned missives at his mother; whose treatment and mistreatment he feels has left him emotionally scarred. The irony is that this is what makes him who he is, someone who feels the pain and anguish of the artist, and maybe, more importantly, the pain and anguish of Black America.

I, too, feel the pain of Black America; for I, too, have felt the pain of black fists and black terror. It is difficult to write about, and I'm not sure this is on track with Eminem and sex, but it does, I feel, explain some of his actions and his ideas, as it does mine. It is with time that they unfold and are expressed through words, which are thrown into the cosmic universe to be captured by..., and I'm stretching, wanting to write "captured by the appropriate ones," but I realize that is not appropriate.

A man with a mullet, his hair in a ponytail, blue hospital scrubs, gray "Members Only" jacket, head on hand leaning to left, elbow on table, a forty something face, looking for words to the crossword puzzle that he eagerly contemplates. All, in black and white...

A birth certificate is also black and white and so is the information contained therein. My birth certificate notes many things: my mother's age, last name and place of birth, for example, and my father's also; their occupations and then information on the newborn—in this case, me—and my mother, "born at sea." And the Marine Drill Instructors were fascinated by that and questioned if my mother was a mermaid. Marine D I's are often amusing when dealing with recruits who, until graduation day, are not called or even considered marines. I was first called "Marine" on April 1, 1983, on Good Friday and it certainly was one, but before that day USMC really could have represented "Uncle Sam's Misguided Children." I will come back to the Corps and to birth certificates, but back to that which is black and white.

Michael Jackson's song "Billie Jean" plays on the Starbucks system. The crowd, both consumers and addicts, is predominantly white, highly affluent, beautiful and very Jewish. It is a chosen place, for chosen people. We, the people are blessed when a tall, stylish, late 40's early 50's black man saunters out of the bathroom as he

American Perversity
Sex, Politics and Religion

snaps his fingers, swinging his arms and shuffling his feet, out the door like so few can, to greet the day. The white skies turn a bit black and the combination becomes gray—as if that mattered.

Another man, an athletic black man, crosses from the corner of Vantage and Ventura, heading north towards Mexicali, his complexion and build like Michael Jordan. He wears blue sweatpants, matching navy blue t-shirt, and sunglasses. He moves with the shopping cart, laden with aluminum, past the Gap and Koo Koo Roo, between Union Bank of California, guiding Ms. "Vons Cart," like an Argentinean tango, down an alley to do his part in keeping California clean, keeping America beautiful. One can at a time...

I just took an hour or so break and walked down to the Kinkos on the corner of Laurel Canyon, and since I'm handwriting this manuscript I need to make copies. I like that word "manuscript," and I prefer writing by hand to the machine. And I listen to the blues and try to think in black and white and I realize that the ladies in gray are thinking in-between because they may be bi-polar, perhaps bi-sexual, and almost certainly lesbians; but maybe not.

The one has been dating long enough to know what she wants and doesn't want, she definitely wants an entrepreneur (I wonder if she thinks writers are entrepreneurs) and now I am sure she is a lesbian and that she is breaking up with her girlfriend as she continues saying that her outside is feminine, but so is her inside. Now, talks of pursuits and pursuing, her masculine side and perceptions.

There are sounds of other patrons, chatter, and light music. Now more words, role-play, dynamic, interesting, something, thinking about, heard or felt from you—I am so stealing their words, ideas and passions. The talker loves being called. They are standoffish with each other. The masculine one sort of grunts, kind-of like a guy, more words, creating ideas, pictures. Masculine to feminine says she pushed her away. The feminine one continues, and says sorry she hurt her.

The broken lesbian rises behind me. I thought to leave, but perhaps to get some sugar to cheer her up. I wonder if she ever called her honey "sugar." Honey is to be preferred, and I sense and hear that the feminine one—the one who wants an entrepreneur—is crying.

31

William Bradford Borden

Starbucks is a great place to break up with someone I would imagine. I had to look and I realize that the chivalrous breaker had brought the mascara-streaked broken, napkins—rougher than tissues—but these are tough girls, California girls, and American girls.

Would they mind if I listened? Do you? Do you listen to yourself? Who does? I think one of the reasons people read less is that they are afraid of silence, afraid of themselves, afraid of the questions. Breaker and broken, no longer on the same current, get up and walk across the street. One leans right up on the window, looking at the cameras, pressing her forehead to the glass, and contemplating the machines, points silently.

Two Jewish men (and when I speak of Jews—and I will much more later in chapter 10, in "AMERICA,"—I speak more in cultural terms than religious ones) sit next to me, replacing the lesbians. Both men are in their late 60s to early 70s, part of the "Greatest Generation," and they are heading toward their final chapters. What have they written? What have they read? One of them wears glasses, his arms crossed. Both are wearing jeans and jean shirts. One for sure is wearing Rockport shoes and the other probably as well. They look like they're in the same military unit.

The one wearing glasses, his mind fully intact, alert and engaged, and nearing his epilogue in life, says to the other attentive, caring one, that he had a beer tonight. Yeah, he was feeling a little depressed. The other, with his baggy eyes, right hand on face, right elbow on table, right pinkie finger with ring, listens attentively while sneaking a beak (and a peak) at two elegant women who enter. And then I hear talk of a daughter, Lauren, having a second child, and a bris, and how they had to come back to Glendale and talk of other people in common.

The man in glasses sips his coffee and then says he would know these people if he saw them, and they relate about relatives, and it seems relative as they head toward the end of their autobiographies, and I am saddened, yet encouraged, when one says he is reading a book. I think it's called *Seabiscuit*, and the talk of war and horses, and there is new energy, new life in death. Maybe that bold bumper sticker on the bumper of the brand-new black Nissan, that I saw as I was driving in to teach this morning proclaiming, "War is not the

American Perversity
Sex, Politics and Religion

answer," maybe they were wrong. And they talk of some sort of horse racing and I am reminded of my birth certificate, which read William Bradford Borden.

Yes, I am William Bradford; my father was William Stephenson, his father William Ross, his father William Wesley, his father William Appleman, all Bordens. My grandfather, William Ross, lost a family fortune gambling, playing cards and owning race horses and gambling on them, and one in particular, a trotter named Mary Gordon, for which he was offered a prince's sum and turned it down, right before the Great Depression, when almost everything was lost. Maybe this book *Seabiscuit*, is about horses and not war. I'm just glad they're reading.

My birth certificate reads, "Place of birth, Kansas City, Missouri." Eminem was also born in Kansas City, on Oct. 17, 1973, which is different than my April 30, 1961. The place is the same, but the date is different. But the date is the same for my brother, Oct. 17. But my brother came 10 years earlier—born in the same place, on the same date, only 3,650 days separating them. They were definitely different times.

Now the man with glasses says the book is about horses is wonderful and then he asserts he doesn't have time for novels, but a friend of his who reads all the time had recommended it. And apparently the woman who wrote the story got it all from the, "horse's mouth," and droopy eyes chuckles and I smile.

I wanted to stop and read back what I had written, but a dapper black man, sport coat and tie, graciously asked if he could borrow the chair and he smiles as I stand up and say "sure," and he walks across to his corner by the counter, pen in hand, writing things down in black and white.

I love listening to the Jewish men talk of war. I think the Jews know something of war. Droopy asserts that he knows that Iraq will execute so-and-so and I feel sorry for calling him droopy eyes. I hope he will not know who he is. Maybe he does and is content with looking kind and educated and ready for the final chapters.

Now talk of past chapters, of Germany, Italy, Japan, of the axis, and the parity of forces and words: production, overabundance, aircraft, P-38s; B-24s; B-29s, and air superiority. And God bless my

33

William Bradford Borden

dear father, the dearest father. Yes, my father who art in the heavens, who would one day rise to vice-president of in-flight service for TWA, where he would serve for more that half of his 65 years. His last take-off was in 1990, and there was no landing. I was there when he took off, soaring like and eagle and I watched as an after-burner of ashes brushed the heavens.

My dad's commute from New Jersey, the Garden State, to New York, the Empire one, was one my dad made for more than 30 years. I wonder how many were on the bus. When I was about three, we left Kansas City for the East Coast. Eminem's family would also leave. They went north, to Detroit, Motor City, Motown, and both of us traded lots of white for black.

As a child, I was afforded the wonderful opportunity and education to travel to Europe, and I vividly remember my love of France. The French could certainly teach the world volumes about style, about food, about passion. I know many Americans think the French are cowards for not supporting us in Gulf II, but we must remember that without their help in Revolutionary times, help that the great Ben Franklin helped ensure, and Franklin, a man of values, 13 that he lived by, 13 that we should study anew. Yes, with the great help of the French, we became a nation.

And the French philosopher, Descartes, espoused in his philosophy, "I think therefore I am," and the story goes that at a faculty party Descartes was asked by the hostess if he would like a glass of wine. Descartes replied, "I think not," and disappeared. There is tremendous power in thought, and in words: active and passive, spoken and heard, written and read.

Eminem knows the power of words and is indeed a modern master, timeless in his scope and reach. I think he reaches left. I don't know if he's a leftist, but I do know he is left-handed. I did my master orals on creativity theory. Left-brain, right-brain properties, are fascinating to me. The word for left in French is "gauche," and in Italian "sinistra" which is the root of sinister. Approximately one in 12 people, less than 10%, is left-handed, but because lefties are much more tapped into their right brains (the artistic side as opposed to the left side, the analytical side, and so it is an inverse, opposite relationship that has been observed significantly through stroke

34

American Perversity
Sex, Politics and Religion

victims) the proportionate legions of lefties in the arts are astronomical.

Think of a few you know as I give you the list. I'll start with an artist in his own right, and several adjectives might be placed before the word "artist" in relation to Bill Clinton. He is a lover of his reading, his country and his countrymen and women—definitely the women. Give him a hand, a left hand.

Other lefties include, from the far right: Ronald Reagan, "The Gipper" #40 who passed off to a quarterback who actually wanted you to read his lips; #41, George W's (#43) father, who is left-handed. He handed off to left-handed (and many felt he conducted his affairs in such manner) running back Clinton (#42) who liked to run behind tight ends. With special breathing techniques, this lefty of lefties, (first far left, then little left, and then nothing...) apparently never inhaled, but I imagine he still loved "Foxy Lady" by Jimi Hendrix and he could relate to that experience.

Hendrix was another lefty. I wonder if he injected the heroin that killed him with his left. I wonder if he had just taken Clinton's lead and just stuck it in, but not injected... But before all of that, in another time in America, at a place called Woodstock, Hendrix would play a haunting electric rendition of "The National Anthem" and it was all part of a new revolution, which 30 or so years later would pass on to Eminem— all in black and white. Maybe it was just a bit shady.

Other lefties, revolutionaries if you will, just a few that I know: Paul McCartney (one of two Beatles left, in what is generally regarded as the greatest rock-and-roll band of all time); Julia Roberts (I thought about choosing her over Jennifer Lopez, a truly "pretty woman," but I felt I needed diversity. Can you affirm that action?). And the list continues, and it is impressive: Matthew Broderick, George Burns, Charlie Chaplin, Tom Cruise, Robert DeNiro, Greta Garbo, Whoopi Goldberg, Betty Grable, Cary Grant, Goldie Hawn, Kermit the Frog, Rock Hudson, Angelina Jolie, Nicole Kidman, Lisa Kudrow, Shirley MacLaine, Steve McQueen, Harpo Marx, Marilyn Monroe, Sarah Jessica Parker (interesting that she and husband Broderick both swing left), Richard Pryor, Robert Redford, Keanu Reeves, Jerry Seinfeld, Dick Van Dyke, Bruce Willis and Oprah Winfrey.

William Bradford Borden

Pretty impressive people and pretty impressive list, and I'll check it twice, left and right. And left to right I write, across the page, top to bottom, left to right, writing down letters, assembling words, creating ideas. I write right, I am white, I am not right because I'm white, nor right because I write; right?

Two cops just came in and they reminded me of a conversation with a New York friend, a professional stuntwoman. A woman whose stream of consciousness is a stream that explodes from her womanhood. Seek out that stream and drink its goodness and bathe in its wonder. And D.G. tells me she's ready to leave New York. The police are everywhere, it feels like a military state, she says. Maybe it is; maybe that is our destiny, our American destiny, and our 21st century destiny. All in the state of our souls, a state of our selves, the Empire State, and yes, the empire is striking back.

Jimi Hendrix was a Vietnam veteran, a cavalry guy, armored cavalry, American cavalry, the baddest, and in a black way "baddest," like hell yeah, and he was a soldier, and he was also one of the greatest, if not the greatest American guitar player and rock-and-roller. The best in a genre that was traditionally white, rock-and-roll, and he would roll it and rock it like so few could, and he was good for those times, when black and white began to mix, when the music became gray, when it all seemed so shady.

Nearly 30 years later, a white messiah, a white messenger, a white prophet would burst onto the scene in the form of Marshall Mathers, Eminem or Slim Shady. I realize that the term "messiah" is explosive in and of itself; the Jews are waiting for theirs, the Christians are waiting for theirs to return, believing he already came in the form of Jesus, a Jew, born in Bethlehem. Could the new messiah have been born in Kansas City, Mo., U.S.A., the "Show Me State," or could this be a false prophet, and I realize how incendiary this all may seem, this talk of sex, politics and religion.

And in the beginning there were slaves, and the slaves were chained, and they were shipped to this new land, this American land. "My country 'tis of thee, sweet land of liberty," and there wasn't. There wasn't justice for all, but there was a sense, I believe, of what could be with time, with trials, with tribulation. Like the Jewish people of a couple millennia before, the blacks were enslaved, chosen

American Perversity
Sex, Politics and Religion

if you will, and their beginning of bondage would sadly often be at the hands of their own brothers who captured them, separated them and sold them—ultimately, transforming the world. Recently there was a book by a respected black academic, which actually argued that slavery had been a blessing for blacks and that the quality of life and the prestige of many, if not most black Americans, is far greater than anywhere in the world.

This is so controversial, I realize, and there is so much I could put down about my own experiences with Black America, for like Eminem who left Missouri, the "Show Me State" for Detroit and Motown, I would leave for the NYC Metro area, for New Jersey, the "Garden State," where I would grow in a garden of all races with a big section of blacks...

Where is this going, this garden metaphor? Perhaps to slavery, and to the fields, and to the sweat and toil of black backs who helped build this country. To the Negro spirituals that they sang and to the rhythm they gave us, and to the juxtaposition of Eminem and Jimi Hendrix; and the irony is that descendants of each could have conceivably been master and slave. And I realize it's a stretch, but somehow I feel a valid one. Master and slave, and the term slave seems so morally reprehensible, and this is a tarnish on our history, but it is also part of what made us great and continues to make us great.

Would we be greater if reparations were made from white to black? I think not. So many whites came after slavery (my maternal grandparents were from England and Norway) and many black Americans themselves, have roots in other places than Africa, the Caribbean for example. Hence I rarely use the term "African American," and hence, in my opinion, the injustice of reparations.

I wonder what our founding fathers would think, many of whom had slaves and many of whom were raised by black women. How lucky they would have been, for there is something so powerful, so maternal, so soulful about a matronly black woman; unfortunately, many of the "masters" took their power to rape and inflict other physical abuses that produced, (something the great Spike Lee often examines in his films—skin color amongst blacks) a varying spectrum of colors and deep resentments.

William Bradford Borden

Do I resent the fact that a friend and I were viciously attacked in high school by three massive black girls who shouted racial epithets when we had walked by and looked in a class where they and a large group stomped their feet and did their drill team thing? Somewhat, but I did retaliate and came close to seriously limiting one's future stomping, after incapacitating one with a hard right to the cheekbones, and then grabbing another and holding her, bending her outside the second floor window and, in my rage, in my anger, in my passion, almost pushing her out, headfirst, 20 feet, down to the concrete.

But I didn't, and I'm glad, and I'm not angry, and maybe she felt better for releasing some of her anger. But I have been there, more than once, and more than most blacks I would imagine. I have been the victim (and no, it is not a one-way street) of racial prejudice, which my black student "Najik" at the college seemed to feel justified and wrote me an angry letter, and gave me a book about the need to break the psychological barriers of slavery, but where is this chapter going? Where is Eminem and where is the sex?

Music is sex; remember the muses and amusement? That is the connection, and I think I will head toward the end of this chapter, toward politics and religion. I must pay tribute again, and again, and again to black people, because they have been such a gain, again and again to my life. From their laughter and love, their insight and observations, their rhythm and their style, their sugar and their souls and I watch them, glad that they are here, glad to hear them, wishing that we mixed more, but happy we brush strokes on our mutual canvas of dreams and desires, as we create a picture, somewhat abstract, often avant-garde, but always changing, always blending and always…

Yesterday, as I drove my car, down Vantage, toward Ventura, the song "We Are Family" jammed from my ride, and a black man, early to mid-50s, walked across to his PT Cruiser, to get something, and I know he heard the music, and I sensed he felt my appreciation, my thanks, and respect, for we are America, brothers and sisters in arms, we are family.

My family has always been there for me, and again, it is difficult to comprehend Eminem's hatred for his mother; although, things were not always completely copasetic with my mother either. It is through

American Perversity
Sex, Politics and Religion

mothers that we enter the world, through mothers that we drink of the milk of the fatted calf. It is through mothers that we often set standards for future relationships; it is a unique, often turbulent ride, the one between mother and son.

I was blessed with a mermaid mom, a Gemini mom, an only child mom of European parents, a greatest generation mom, a mom who is very involved with her Episcopal church, yet counts Jews amongst her very best friends—a mom who has guided me and often, I think, felt slighted by my actions and inactions. A mom whom I have burdened and anguished in the past, a mom that I now want to honor and cherish (and in a way always have), a mom that I am proud of, a mom that I want to be proud of me. She bore me, a Borden, and the Borden company had a slogan, an ad campaign, that said "If it's Borden, it has to be good" and I'm trying, but I realize the trying times and I share a letter she wrote me on the day of my graduation, after I returned from my time in the desert, my time in the wilderness, my time apart.

Dear Brad,   June 20, 1979
     Congratulations on your high school graduation. May it lead to another four years from now. At an occasion such as this it would seem appropriate to look back over the years to examine where you've been and then to look ahead to see where you are going.
     Up until now, you've had our full support and backing, but it would seem you no longer need your family. You had no choice into what family you were born into, as we too, took potluck with what that birth would produce.
     We have tried to instill in our children certain moral and ethical standards both through example and instruction. Last year you tested these standards and put yourself and us through a catharsis. For a time it seemed that our value system had won, but apparently that isn't the case at least not yet. You seem to need to test our system and more importantly yourself. Fortunately you hold yourself in high esteem (arrogant

William Bradford Borden

could also be used) and have the confidence to succeed.

Since you want to do everything your way, I feel my role as a mother is now over and you may go out on your own to become or do whatever you want or can. If you ever find that you can accommodate yourself to my standards I'll be happy to assist in any way.

In the meantime, I wish you happiness and good luck and I hope you may be spared the pain and anguish you have put us through.

With love,
Mom

With love mom to you, I thank you. Thank you for instilling your values in me; yes, I know you don't agree with what you perceive as my "womanizing" ways, but I think it's a bit hypocritical because you've always been such a big supporter of Clinton; and so I am fairly certain that marriage is not for me, nor perhaps Wild Bill, or Marshall.

The state of the family and marriage in Black America has been the object of discussion of sociologists for some time. The number of black families headed by mothers is proportionally much greater than those of their white counterparts, as are their numbers in prison, where we have locked away a generation of black males...all, in White America.

"White America" is the name of an Eminem piece. Here's a white man, from the "Show Me State," growing up in Detroit, in Motown and experiencing the black culture to a far, far greater extent than the majority of White America.

I would think to be a black male in America, more so than a black female, would be a daily struggle, one that I could not begin to comprehend, but one I will attempt to understand. And I realize comprehend and understand are so close, as are sympathy and empathy and so I will look at the nuances, like the ever-changing colors of Michael Jackson in the chapter he shares with Michael Jordan, all from my perspective. A white one...I am certainly not advocating a White America, in fact I feel extremely blessed to have,

American Perversity
Sex, Politics and Religion

for the majority of my life, lived on one coast or another, where the spectrum of the rainbow is more intense and where the sunrises and sunsets are much more pronounced.

42

SEXSOME II: POLITICS

44

4
Earth Mother

Thanks to Oprah Winfrey, many millions have begun to read again and to form book clubs and to discuss ideas, and words, and each other. In the year 2000, around the time many Americans started to panic about the potential problems posed by Y2K, there were many programs that celebrated various influential people, "best of" lists if you will, in areas like history, music and sports. This book is a type of "top 10" list. As the clock ticks, the pages turn and life is written.

"Oprah" backwards would be Harpo, and Harpo was one of the Marx Brothers. The Marx brothers were Jewish immigrants who were instrumental in the transition and transmission of Jewish culture, thought and ideals from vaudeville to theatre to television and film. I wonder if the Marx brothers were Marxist.

I am not a Marxist, but Marx, wrote two things that I think are most relevant. And what is relevant to me might not be relevant to you, but isn't all that relative and aren't we all relatives? Relatively speaking, that is. And Marx wrote, "Religion is the opiate of the masses," and, "Work expands to fill the time."

Oprah, I imagine, loves her job. She seems to revel in her work, her artistry, and her pathos. Unfortunately, so few of us do love what we do. Maybe if values and goals were more readily established, we would. I just realized why I am so enjoying this writing process. Writing is in the moment; each letter comes at that time, which is now, always now, time won, won now, now—one on one.

45

William Bradford Borden

The Jews and Chinese, amongst others, have other calendars besides our Western one. This gets back to the concept of math and time, and how the work or activities are often expanded to fill it. Wouldn't it be wonderful to fill time with wonder and joy and heaven on earth; but what is heaven without hell? What is a vacation without work? What is life without death?

Organized religions usually have some sort of explanation for life after death. It is interesting to note that many of these philosophies come from the relatively ancient past. Many religions contend that the earth was created and man came into existence in the last 5,000 years. But, aren't dinosaurs just fascinating? That's ancient past, a past that many ancient religions want to deny.

Those dinosaurs became fossils, and then fuel, and then the "fuelers" ran out of gas. I wonder if they called it gas, way back then in Iraq, the cradle of civilization, home of Baghdad, Ancient Babylon, and the Tigris and Euphrates? These beasts, woolly mammoths and mastodons alike, gave power to our modern beasts, our Hummers, our Bradley Fighting Vehicles, our jet airplanes.

Then, one day, the fossil fuel fueled one plane, then another. Two planes, and the destination, the objective was two towers, symbols, much like Gemini, the twins. Side-by-side they stood. They held their ground; but, the flying pterodactyls, full of ancient liquid approached. Side-by-side they flew. And the man-made beasts pierced the brother and then the sister and their stomachs vomited fuel and fire. And the towers were a perfect Empire State couple, but named for the world. And they were meant for trade, for commerce, for creation. Instead, they became a center of cremation—how sad, how ancient, how prophetic...

How prophetic, and prophecy only works if you believe, and is only apt if what you have chosen to believe comes to fruition. Yes, most certainly we are known for our fruits, so stop blaming Eve for the whole garden, tree of knowledge apple thing. I think many of us our afraid of knowledge, afraid of the garden, and afraid of ourselves.

I wonder if Marx was afraid when he proclaimed, "Religion is the opiate of the masses." Do you believe what religious texts tell you? Or do you believe in those who tell you what to believe? Do you believe what is written in the Bible?

American Perversity
Sex, Politics and Religion

The 46th Psalm (which is double the 23rd that I read at my father's funeral, and begins "The Lord is my shepherd; I shall not want...") is quite fascinating. The 46th word, in the King James Version, from the top is "Shake." It is interesting to note that some people think that Shakespeare may have helped in the publishing of the *King James Bible* that came out when Shakespeare was around 46, and so it is not surprising, or is it, that the 46th word from the bottom of the 46th Psalm is "spear." How is this relevant to Oprah? I guess I'm just trying to make a point.

Oprah Winfrey was born at home in Kosalusko, Miss., on January 29, 1954. That means many things: one that she is an Aquarian and this is the Age of Aquarius, and another, that she will be 50 in 2004. Oprah Gail Winfrey once credited her existence to a "one-day fling under an oak tree." How profound that this child of an 18-year-old maid and a 20-year-old father would go on to achieve the greatness that she has.

Her first years were spent on her grandmother's Mississippi farm, but by the time Oprah was six she moved to Milwaukee to live with her single mom. Raped at nine by a teenage cousin and then molested by three other men, "friends of the family," over the next five years, she left Wisconsin to live with her father, a barber. Barbers, like beauticians, often seem more capable than many psychotherapists, because they literally work with the head. In a more metaphysical sense, they often have a better understanding of how to exact change and create possibility. There is most certainly a great deal of group therapy going on in America's salons and barbershops.

With her father's guidance and direction, the 5'7" Oprah, went from a problem student to honor student, from low self-esteem to being voted the most popular student at Nashville High School and competing in the Miss Black America pageant. Winning a scholarship to Tennessee State University for oratory, she graduated in 1971 with a degree in speech and drama. While still in college, she took a job as a broadcaster on a local TV station.

I turn the channel on another day and I realize that the TV has become an IV, a constant drip. Like the drip of coffee, the drip of oil, the drip of blood, the TV drips into the consciousness of the world. I have never seen Oprah's show. Today is Sunday and I've written in

47

William Bradford Borden

my Franklin Day Planner, named in honor of Ben Franklin, to check her out tomorrow.

Millions watch Oprah every day. Her show is aired all over the world. I like that "air" thing, I think, ironically enough that in this age of Aquarius that Oprah is part of the Aquarian tribe; interesting, isn't it, that there are 12 tribes of Israel, 12 signs of astrology and 12 apostles? The master chef must have had a party in mind with her baker's dozen. *Bon appetit*!

The Aquarian "tribe" is not (which is strange considering the root "aqua") a water sign. The three water signs are Cancer, Pisces, Scorpio, and they go best with the three earth signs, Capricorn, Taurus, and Virgo. The four elements (and there are three each of the four primary elements, which are the essence of who we are) are water, earth, fire and air. The fire signs: Sagittarius, Aries and Leo, go best with the air signs: Gemini, Aquarius and Libra. Could one believe in all three tribes—in Israel, the apostles, and astrology? I know, or at least that is what a book once said, that at least one of the 12 had one who was false. How obscure.

Such obscure references—I think you may think, if you think— and patronizing tone. I'm sorry. I want this book to be balanced, contemplative and controversial. I want people to think when they read it. I want to think, that by thinking, we are, and we are what we think. Drip, drip, drip...

What's in the air? Michael Jackson, singing he wants to rock with me. In the air I hear his voice. Yesterday, Jessica Lynch was in the air, and now she is at Walter Reed Army Medical Center, which is in Washington, D.C. (and talk about a place that is electrically charged, full of megawatt power and light). Walter Reed is named for the scientist who dealt with malaria that was dealt by mosquitoes, who fly, like Delta, in Atlanta, like CNN, which is on the air, like Oprah, which I'm going to watch tomorrow, on the 14th of April 2003.

There is a lot in the air, in the Age of Aquarius, and certainly Oprah Winfrey is heir apparent, if not ruler on the throne of the spiritual power of women, the archetypal Earth Mother: Cassandra, prophetess, and seer.

How can I make this pronouncement on a show that I've never seen, on a show that is seen in more than 100 countries and has been

American Perversity
Sex, Politics and Religion

number one for upwards of 20 years? Because I have witnessed the subtle but major, major but subtle, changes in black and white, White and Black America, and I appreciate, understand and acknowledge Oprah's inestimable contribution.

I am excited about tomorrow's show. I wonder what message Oprah will have for me. Isn't that what a seer does? They see, through the air, through the wind, through the breath and I hear in the air a Rolling Stones song about time not waiting for anyone, and I realize they too—my English brothers—are also prophets. False ones, some might say, and how sad to think this of the Stones, who along with Eminem have been the greatest musical emissaries of white to black. Much like Oprah Winfrey and Colin Powell have been emissaries of black to white.

Yes, it may well be the Age of Aquarius, but I imagine, and yes, John Lennon a messenger himself imagining, "all the people…" And I think of the three that are 12, the apostles, the signs, and the tribes, imagine, "living life in peace." The process itself has become so profound in this age of invaders and infidels: Aquarians and space travelers; Israel and Palestine, Palestine, Israel that is; unfortunately, no liquid gold. Who sold them that real estate?

Oprah's real estate must be most impressive, for she is herself most impressive and I think she deserves to live like a queen: a voluptuous, Rubenesque goddess. I think it would be cool to see her home in an MTV Cribs way, and I was going to note earlier that I write "an" MTV because "M" is pronounced with an "Eminem" type sound, but I was making my grammatical disclaimer. Anyway, wouldn't you like to see Oprah's crib, her pad, her domain? She is our royalty and, yes, she speaks our language. But she also speaks through the air, through America, through the world. She speaks the language that flows through the oceans, crawls along the beaches, burns the jungles and whips the tornados. She speaks the language of today.

Politics…I think this is supposed to be in the section on politics and, in fact, this is where Oprah belongs. Who am I to say where someone belongs, or is that ironically enough what politics is, a series of choices and decisions to choose who decides? Did you decide to vote and whom are you voting for? Certainly the world has shifted

49

William Bradford Borden

from a geo-political world to a geo-economic one, and certainly Oprah's empire is an economic one, driven by advertising and advertisers that send their own message and messages.

The message we are sending is that big business, economics and money do business with politicians who try to sell us what we may or may not need, creating activity to re-create in mass what has been created by a few. But the game-keepers must keep the mass, the ones that re-create instead of recreate, keep them in the maze and in the race, just so they can have a couple of days a week to rest, to pray, and consume. But it is the creators who choose, the creators who decide, and the creators who invent themselves.

In the inventory of life there are so few true creators, for we have been told, "Many are called but few are chosen." Could there be more creators? Absolutely, and that would be fabulous, but so many are too busy reinventing themselves, reconstructing the past or planning for the future that they aren't able to be in the present, to be in the moment, to be in the now and create.

In the air yesterday, I heard one of my senior students say, under her breath, a breath of air; I heard the wise whisper that she expressed. I was afraid of commitment. Could I be faithful? I could certainly be full of faith and that is why I am confident, ("con" with, "fidelis" faith) yes, *fidelis*, faith, *semper fidelis*, always faithful; yes, of that I am confident, I am with faith.

Today, on the 14th of April, I saw the show for the first time, I saw Oprah, number one for 20 years, showing the rest of the world America's number two export, and that's entertainment. And by God New York if you can make it there... But how about paying the policemen and firemen, the teachers and soldiers more? They are on the forefront of defending and upholding the rights and privileges of you—and I don't want to sound elitist—but, you who are reading these words. I hope the common man will read them too, but too many of them, serving you, are so exhausted at the end of the day that all they can do is read the paper, listen to Mariah, or watch Oprah.

Today on "Oprah," the first day I've ever seen the show, today, the special guest was Mariah Carey. Mariah Carey, like Halle Berry, has a white mother. If Halle Berry is the first "African American" woman to win Best Actress, then what happened to her mom? Aren't

American Perversity
Sex, Politics and Religion

we talking about a 50/50 love Teddy P.? That's Pendergrass, that's soul, that's a black thing; and yes, I understand. I was alluding to a Teddy Pendergrass song that settles, like a seesaw, soulfully with a 50/50 love.

And so we have—like the letters that you read on the paper that you hold—it's all black and white, and with that mixture, the gray matter (and it does matter), the gray of the black and white. The gray of the white and black, black letter, black power, impressing you, touching you, impregnating you with the letters that rub your bark, your wood, your white soul, the 26 letters create words, create sentences, create paragraphs, create ideas. And there must be relevance if the seconds, the minutes, the hours like sand coming down the hourglass, like semen, microscopic sperm, overfilling you in the daily climax of life, and indeed, "So are the days of our lives."

Who decides if this book is published may ultimately fall to one of the members of one of the 12 tribes. The ones that decided to make President Bush the president, by certain misdirection, as the Palm Beach Holocaust Jews, misguidedly selected ultra right-winger Pat Buchanan in the first edition butterfly ballot, replete with hanging "chads" that some thought fortuitously, providentially, bizarrely, as if with divine guidance gave Bush Florida—president that is—gave honor back, many thought, to the White House.

Gave the Jews, who had suffered "the slings and arrows of outrageous fortune" often at much more than a pound of flesh, these chosen ones, chose (and so many of those who had been chosen were no longer left to choose) the man, the Yankee man, the Texas man, the American, who would ride into Washington with his armored cavalry and give those chosen, those in Florida, many with tattoos on their arms, tattoos, not of love, not of passion, not of words, but of numbers. Those people who sent a mandate with a Bush as their governor and now Bush as their president. There would be no beating around it. They had been beaten all their lives and their bush was burning, and their mandate to the world was that it was not the one written in Numbers only. That was obvious, the power of numbers, of math of mastery. But the mandate was written in books—their Torahs, their Talmuds and their Testaments (the Old one the original, not the New one, the sequel).

William Bradford Borden

And the Jews knew what to do. They knew the gray of crematorium sunrises, crematorium sunsets, and crematorium nightmares. They also knew the power of now, the power of sunrises, won over Masada, when an ancient tribe decided to return to a land, a chosen land, a biblical land. And the mandate they sent was already written and their script was already being directed in America, in New York and L.A., in Washington and Missouri, in Texas and Florida, directed by the chosen, chosen to decide—decided to be chosen. It was a choice many would regret. They knew false prophets and their messages.

The messages and the message of the people today, tax day, the 15th day of the fourth month, of the 2,003 years since another tax day on the birthday of a carpenter, of a director, of a creator, in Bethlehem, in Israel, in a manger. And the stars were bright and stardom was chosen for the role of a lifetime, role of the world, the role of messenger, of prophet, of Jew.

Now a model pitches, producer creates and the masses recreate. Hocus pocus, and yet, it is what it is, because we are, who we are. Or maybe, more definitively, of what we are because it is written. I wish model would go. Like a young child, she is meant to be seen and not heard, to speak when spoken to, but I want to hear what is written, what the producer creates.

Shakespeare, like almost all great storytellers, "stole" his ideas, his plots and his thoughts from other people, cultures, and stories. What made Shakespeare so omnipotent lies in the title of the magnificent work by Harold Bloom, *Shakespeare, The Invention of the Human*. And what made Shakespeare the master of his craft were words, words, and words…kind of like location, location, location for real estate, or…

Another book, by another Bloom, Alan, talks about the disappearance of the Western canon; although, Western cannons sure have been appearing a lot recently; and, if you're not familiar with the difference, then you're probably not familiar with the canon that is Western, and heavily, proportionately, dead European white males, and it has suffered horrifically. Shot with the cannon of political correctness, and in the process of correcting things politically, we have the crux of Alan Bloom's must-read, *The Closing of the*

American Perversity
Sex, Politics and Religion

American Mind. I wonder what Oprah will recommend when she returns to the classics. I hope she's correct. Her selections will certainly be political.

The story I was originally going to call the "Mariah Carey story," but due to political correctness, will now be called "The story formerly to be called the Mariah Carey story." How princely, you might think. It is a story that encourages you to think.

Once upon a time (and you can leave that out if you recount the tale) there was a young girl who was 10 and she wanted her father to read to her. She loved *The Giving Tree*, but later she would come to believe the message was really misogynistic and the female tree was giving everything, life and limb, to satisfy the man. But at that point she still loved the tale and so she begged her dad to read.

The father was watching the Jets play the Giants (great names for New York teams; yes Jets, and Giants), who were playing at their home in New Jersey, and the father wanted to continue watching the game. He was sick of the tree story; he already knew how to manipulate women and his daughter was no different. So, he picked up a *National Geographic,* and from the magazine the father pulled out a map of the world. He ripped it into about 100 pieces and gave it to his young daughter, instructing her to return when the newly created puzzle was completed.

The father went back to drinking his beer and was pleased that he would finish the first half of the game. The daughter returned about 15 minutes later and the puzzle was complete. The father was astounded, "How did you do that?" he questioned his daughter, who told him the secret, and the secret was...

"If you turn the world over there is a picture of a man on the other side, and if you put the man together, the world will take care of itself."

In the world we have many choices and decisions and that is often the basis for advertisers who advertise their products. Products and advertising and the choice to watch and consume are what have driven Oprah to her destination—a product that is desired. Advertisers, with their products, pay a small fortune to have their products used and displayed in film and television.

William Bradford Borden

I prefer the human parade—much more evident on the streets of London, Paris and New York—to the scripted, acted and directed one. And I'm reminded of a bumper sticker I saw in Haight Ashbury, San Francisco, which was the center of the Summer of Love in '68; and I drove for Jerry Garcia and the Grateful Dead, and I think I will start dropping names and showing you the six degrees of separation, which was the name of a film which I'm sure had product placement, and the bumper sticker aptly read and I connected with the idea: "Theatre is art, film is life, and television is furniture."

Talk about tangents, or rather read what I have written, and then talk of them and I don't know where the young wannabe product, ready to be placed went. I didn't get to see her slink out the door in her blue sweat suit with the bold letters "Juicy" on her ass. I'm sure the pronouncement is correct. She looks ripe and fresh. Definitely juicy, no false advertising there and I'm totally behind her product.

The "juice" at Starbucks is coffee and I hear someone request a "venti drip." I guess it's better than an I.V. drip, and then the requisite, "Have a good day..." and I'm sure he will. I wonder what is on "Oprah" today. I will get back to the one and only show I saw, the one with Mariah, not the Mariah Story, but the Mariah episode. But last night when I got home from a Passover Seder, I watched a bit of the film *Beloved*, and was so impressed with Oprah. The film was produced by her company, Harpo Productions, so I guess my opening salvo, in allusion to the Marx brothers was not very original. What is, William, what is? I hope my language, insights and observations are. And the word "are" is the second person singular of the verb "to be" and "are" is also the plural (we are, you are, they are) of the verb "to be"... "To be or not to be..." that is always the question. "To be or not to be..." is always the quest.

The quest for stardom, for fame, for actors, often begins on Broadway, or off, or even "off off." Broadway is also known as the Great White Way. Broadways is also the name of a department store where they sell products—which are placed on shelves—and maybe books like this, but Broadway, the former, is in the most powerful city in the world, in New York City. The theatre would rumble and roar if Oprah took the stage in the role of Ruth in Lorraine Hansberry's amazing play *Raisin in the Sun*, which in my opinion is an equally

American Perversity
Sex, Politics and Religion

powerful vision of the American dream, to Arthur Miller's *Death of a Salesman*. It is one that belongs in the canon of great literature. It is one that Oprah should produce and star in. It is one she should promote as a true classic.

A classic cast and production, which could run for years, although the actors probably couldn't, but then could be re-made into a film, would be with the following cast and crew. Oprah, with Harpo Productions, would produce and Ossie Davis would direct. Ossie's wife, Ruby Dee, would play Momma; Oprah as Ruth; Denzel as Walter, Halle as Beneatha; Seal as Assagai, Chris Rock as George Murchison; and I as Lidner.

Wow! What a production it would be. I was thinking of Matthew Broderick for the role of Lidner, but I would be so honored to play the painful but pivotal role of the only white man in the play—a role that would seep my soul because of his covert racism. But I would be honored to have a role in *Raisin in the Sun*, one of the greatest American dramas, performed by some of the greatest African American actors in America, on Broadway, the Great White Way, New York City.

What way am I taking with this work? What direction, what course? If someone intervenes in the middle of your course, is that intercourse? Or, do we get fucked on a regular basis, sometimes enjoying it and sometimes not? New York got fucked, for want of a better word, and I don't want a better word right now. "Fucked" is totally appropriate. New York got fucked. Then again, New York fucks a lot; there are a lot of fuckers in New York—a whole United Nations of fuckers. Is it better to give than to receive? I guess that depends on what stand you take. Of course, you could always change your position.

I have been writing so much lately. It is a feeling of immortality. But how would one know or feel of immortality if one had never tasted death? I have, many, many times. And we will all dine of death and I forced myself to write that. We joke about death, and cry about death, we avoid death. We are scared to death, do death-defying thinks, and I wrote thinks instead of things, and I wanted to wax eloquent on death, but then I think of Madame Tussaud's, and those famous enough to be waxed for public fondling, schmoozing

William Bradford Borden

and photographing. Best friends for a moment with William and Diana, Elvis and Arnold. Three dead, but one is still terminating. And when will this chapter end or, rather, when will your chapter end; where did it begin? And the metaphor shifts from dining and salivating, to writing and publishing. What will you publish and what have you written? And, once again, where do you stand?

The towers stood side by side, and in New York, white and black rub shoulders much more than in most of America, and I had that blessing in New Jersey, being touched by angels, blacks and Jews.

Across the gap is a parade of product looking to be placed, looking for their place in the sun, and yes, Langston Hughes, "What happens to a dream deferred?"

Now, more products cross south, rather from the south, across the boulevard, north to Mexicali. And I look left to the Gap, and the advertisers are ahead of me. The proclamation proclaims, "black and white is blooming." I guess if you're filling the gap, that's true. It's Good Friday; spring is in the air; Michael Jordan no longer is, and much is left to be written.

A 30-something black man sits with a script at the green outdoor Starbucks table, wearing a blue N.Y. Yankee cap. And we sit, side by side, filling the gap with conversation, talking of cars, of basketball, of women, side by side, two men, black and white, blooming in the sun, California sun—sons of America. He smokes a cigar and contemplates things, maybe the women, when he tells me he just keeps the conversation low, and there aren't enough rich men for all the beauties. And he and I are ready, willing and able to fill the gaps of the daughters of the revolution, Hollywood women, American women, and the parade continues on Friday, Good Friday.

Last Monday, on the 14th, I watched Oprah and her guest Mariah (who was herself the product of black and white blooming in the gap) and she began with a song, after Oprah had introduced her as the biggest selling female artist of all time, the winner of two Grammy's. And the song—perhaps a cry for some much needed nourishment—for serious blooming, was called "Through the Rain" and Oprah sang along. She's certainly weathered a few storms in her life.

When the song is over they sit and talk and Mariah tells Oprah that the song is a metaphor for life. Oprah says to her, "You write all

American Perversity
Sex, Politics and Religion

your songs; you really rich," and she's most certainly right, because writing and publishing, not recording, is where the money is. Mariah, equally prepared, sharing public knowledge, "ah hahs" back and says, "We know who has all the money," to which Oprah replies, "Okay, we both rich." Indeed they are, and enrich us they do, Oprah Woman, Mariah Woman, "ah ha" women.

Oprah feels that "Through the Rain" sounds like an anthem of spirituality, and then she goes right to common knowledge regarding Mariah, the breakdown, Mariah's story, not the Passover story, and Oprah doesn't let it pass, and she questions, staccato the probe, "So tell us what happened…" and Mariah fires back, "I was exhausted."

Oprah and Mariah, Mariah and Oprah, both agree they are workaholics, and Oprah shares, "It's even harder when you love your work." Oprah and Mariah, the best of the best, moving through the rain, sensual and wet and Oprah is empathetic, a good listener, leaning forward, picking up mirrors, razor sharp, like a psychologist, lessons learned from her father, the barber, I imagine.

Mariah shares her experience that happened a couple of days before her breakdown, and a clip is shown with her on a cable show, *TRL*, and the clip shows a sensual, semi-striptease by Mariah and her body is burning, smoking, needing some heavy, heavy rain to get inside to quench her fire…

And I want to see more of Mariah; I want to do a duet with her, and do my own striptease. I want to strip her, and be stripped and strip away the layers, the lust and lies. I want to call her master and for her to call me slave. I want to feel her body, want to feel her pain, to touch her spirit; I want to be her dream lover, and her hero. I want to carry her away, to carry Mariah with care, and give her a package that I can put inside, in the gap, where it's warm and safe. A black box, Pandora's Box, Mariah's box, and 270 days later, I want to be present, to open the box, right at the crucial gap. To hear her sing, sing to the gift, and for the gift, melody and harmony, black and white, blooming baby, blooming…

As impressed with Oprah and Mariah as I was, that was all of the show I watched. I did, however, wait for the commercials, to look at the products to see how the placements have helped to place Oprah on the throne of daytime. Instead of the drugs, which are pushed in the

57

William Bradford Borden

evening, during the news, these were different products for different people, for different users. The pushing amazed me—amazed at the products—givers and takers, taking and giving.

There were a total of nine commercials by my count, and I'm sure they counted for the product placers. The nine began: first with maids, merry ones; then Sears, with the lowest price of the season, "Sears, where else?" then to Hallmark, for Easter cards "they'll never forget" (what if they're forgotten?). Next Reach Max (not like it's a robbery, but Reach Max to prevent gum disease). Then crackers, you got to promote crackers. Crackers love Oprah and Oprah probably loves crackers, but I wonder if she loves the Ritz ones she pushes, Garlic Ritz crackers.

That's just the middle of the products pushed, 5 of 9, and people are working 9 to 5 to buy them, consuming and consumed; and I am exhausted just watching, thinking of becoming a workaholic like Oprah and Mariah, so I could afford a maid, a card, a cracker, afford to be a parent, and it is apparent that many cannot afford to be parents, but can we afford not to be? And the next commercial will show you how to raise kids if you call 1-800kids something. Next, I am invited down to Mervyns, where "prices are down and there are big brands and small prices"; and finally, and now I count eight as opposed to nine, and eight is certainly enough, and the final is for "Piglet's Big Movie" and I just can't wait to see that one.

A white, wheel-chair-bound woman, 40-something, probably younger but looking older, and she looks like one of those women in the Depression era, dustbowl, black and white photos, and she is with two daughters, pre-teens, pushing teens, pushing mom. They are trailer park types, the kind that would like Oprah and, more importantly, have time to watch, and she asks me for some money, and I check and I only have one 10 and one 20. And I am hurting, deficit spending, but so is she. And they wheel away and I feel guilty; and so, I follow, east they go toward Jerusalem.

They turn in at the Barnes and Noble Bookstar, down the alley where books become stars. And I call to them and they stop. And the older, dirty-blonde daughter takes the 10 and thanks me and says God bless; yes, God Bless America I think. And I go up to the mom, and I see on the left side of her neck the name "David"—an advertisement

American Perversity
Sex, Politics and Religion

perhaps—in permanent ink. And I wonder if David is her king, and she also blesses me, for God, and she hands me a paper. A message, not from God, but "Diet Magic," but it doesn't look like it's working for her. Maybe her last supper will be sooner than she expects, as she rolls away on her home office.

What is work? Is it completely necessary for all of us, for America and the U.S.? Certainly, there is credence in Oprah's commentary on the workaholic and how it's even harder when you love what you do. In America, in social settings, upon initial meetings, the first question we often ask, in quest of a better understanding of one another, we ask, "What do you do?" What do you do? ("To be or not to be..." "To do or not to do..." So the verb "to do" becomes a sister of "to be," in the pursuit of action, power and destiny.) "Do you take..." and the operative word is "take," we are takers. Sometimes givers, but always takers, as some official in uniform, officiating, asks the players, the dramatist, the actors, "Do you take..." the script is written, and the tired response is "I do..." Of course they do. They know the answer. They've heard it all their lives. But, do they know the question?

My Franklin Planner is open before me, and I have personified him, and call him Franklin, and at the top of the page, in sea green, under a compass, a question asks, "Are the things you value most governing your decisions?" And I remember a couple of weeks ago when my college freshmen sat in a circle and we talked of values. I felt proud to be their teacher, proud to facilitate and educate and, at the end, a student questioned me and asked what my values were. I thought for just a moment and answered and gave them "love." Love is a good thing to give; it is a good thing to get, giving and receiving.

Next to the question, "Are the things you value most governing your decisions?" there is a quote from Pearl S. Buck that reads: "The secret of joy in work is contained in one word: excellence. To know how to do something well is to enjoy it." There is so much truth in that, and you can see how joyful Oprah appears to be and the joy she brings others—rising every day, working and celebrating, a job well done. Yes, well done, you good and faithful servant. Servant no more, you are the master, master of the universe. Thank you, beloved Oprah.

60

5
Black Magic

It is Easter evening, April 20, 2003. And the day is done; and I will—because this is the beginning of Chapter 5—get to the point. There won't be the freedom there was with Oprah. Oprah, the earth mother, creates that feeling. And so I will go right away to the *Taps story*, a north/south story, a black/white story, and an American story. This is an appropriate transition, I believe. And isn't belief such a powerful force? Or perhaps beliefs are forced to be powerful; a transition from Oprah to two Michaels, one Jackson, and one across Jordan, one north/south, one east/west, one black one white, one America.

The *Taps story* is a story of the Civil War—the Greatest War ever fought—an American War. And Americans are warriors; we are built on a war culture. Just look at our holidays, our cities, our exports, and there is a pre-Taps story that I remember distinctively reading from that woman with the most intelligent IQ, the ask Marilyn Von Something. And I'd love to have a prodigy with her, and the prequel is about having children, civil children, American children—Yankees and 'Rebs'...

There were no cruise missiles during the Civil War; although, that is not completely correct. The Native Americans (and let's stop calling them Indians. That's Gandhi, the Taj Mahal, and yoga) had tomahawks and threw them like missiles; these razor-sharp axes cruising through Northern and Southern skylines, straight to their

William Bradford Borden

target. Right between the eyes they flew. Tomahawk cruise missiles—American ingenuity.

Back to the story; and the story isn't so much about the Native Americans, who are certainly involved, but about Europeans. And many would call them invaders—the mostly White Anglo-Saxon Protestants who re-located massive numbers of Africans. They were brought to the South to grow tobacco, to smoke out Europe, to light a fire under America. Their parentage, mothers and fathers were abused and murdered, givers and receivers—former slaves.

Many say that the Civil War was fought primarily over slavery. That is not completely—or in many respects—remotely correct. Check out on your own the reasons. Somewhere it has been said that the winners write the history books. Have you read any losers lately?

American men are—by nature, and compared with the majority of the rest of the world; excluding, perhaps Africa—in many respects, more primitive than most of the industrialized world (and I realize most of Africa is far from industrialized). Primitive people, our roots are transplanted from the rest of the world, and so the seedlings come and come, fertilizing each other, fertilizing the earth, fertilizing our mother, America. And the new plants, the new hybrids...the new genus, is a magnificent, aromatic, powerful weed, bush or flower— there is such power in flowers—flower power.

The *Marilyn von Civil War Story* is this, "If the approximately 620,000 soldiers who died in the Civil War had not died (and more soldiers died in the Civil War than in all the other U.S. wars combined), what would the population of America be now?" The answer from this Genius, this Marilyn...

I would love to lie in bed with the Genius Von Marilyn, after entering her soul (I just wondered if I should make a PG13 version of this book), after sharing her air and devouring her creative juices. I think I'll bring her a hot pink flannel *PRINSEX* set, form-fitting her ass, and she would talk about O.J., the case and lawyers. "Little gators," she might call them, and then she might say she could play Nicole and I could play O.J.

But then she changes her mind. "Not appropriate," she whispers lustily, her nipples piercing my stomach, and I wonder if she does one-on-one sessions, or maybe she likes groups. "Sexual Healing"

American Perversity
Sex, Politics and Religion

plays on the radio, and she says, "You play Chris Darden, and I'll play Marcia Clark," and I bend her over and spank her juicy ass, the flannel providing a bit of comfort. And she is comforting, consoling, cajoling, as she bends over, enjoying being disciplined, the naughty head mistress, always at the head, sucking up the knowledge, engulfing it, swallowing it whole.

There are several holes—just not in her argument. And Von Marilyn, this symbol of perfection, of beauty, of genius, the ultimate Muse—her Medusa-like hair framing her face, framing the highest IQ, the face of an angel. But the candlelight presents a devil, a vixen, a temptress; her holes are wet and so is my appetite, and as I rip her sweat pants off her juicy ass she wrestles herself away, laughing and crying, and she unleashes a golden torrent over me and I am warmer, surprised and delighted, and she says, "It's not what you think." And I take her into the shower and sit her in the tub, the pulsing jets hitting my back, and I am full of life, of power, of the moment, and I shower her. It is a golden moment. Thanks for the peace, and ohm, yes ohm...

So, back to reality...and the answer to the *Vos* (not *Von*), the *Vos Marilyn Story* of the Civil War, and the answer. Most people guess that the population would have doubled in the almost 140 years since the war ended and the million men marched no more, and that answer seems somewhat reasonable. Look at the populations of India (the home of true Indians—the originals—and soon to surpass China as the most populous) and China (start checking out your electronic equipment, silverware, clothing, and even the kid in the carriage being pushed by the white parents. Do you care? "Made in China," populating the world with products); but that is not the answer. What is the question, you might be musing, do you need to ask, ask yourself?

The answer is, according to Ms. Genius—I wonder what she told her classmates when they teased her, "You think you're so smart..."

Marilyn Vos Savant. Savant is her last name; is that where they get that Savant title or am I an idiot? Maybe, instead of OJ/Nicole, which we decided not to play, in favor of Chris and Marcia (Darden and Clark), maybe we should play Marilyn and Joe, or Marilyn and Jack, or Marilyn and Bobby—where have they gone? Three of four

William Bradford Borden

retired early; no more "Happy Birthdays to you." Have you thought about retirement? What about entitlement? Is any of this relevant?

In the post-Civil War—or rather current America—United States that is (and, really, how united are we? Pretty damn, I'd say. North and south, black and white, east and west, hot and cold, blue and gray, peaceniks and warriors, blondes and brunettes, Botox and blowjobs, Muslim and Jew, Puritan and pornographer, hip hop and jazz, baseball and basketball, Harleys and Hooters, rappers and panderers, masters and slaves, products and placement, summer and winter, fall and spring, rich and poor, living and dead, beaches and mountains, canyons and shores, N.Y. and L.A., melody and harmony. That's right ring, ding, dong…) the population would be…

I guess all the ringing, dinging and donging wouldn't have mattered much because the population would be virtually the same as it is today if those 620,000 men had not died during the Civil War.

Here is the power of women and why we don't send them into combat… One man can conceivably (and "conceive" is the operative word) impregnate an almost infinite number of women. A million sperm go a long way. Women, therefore, go a long way—nine months, from start to finish, producing a product that, in turn, takes a lifetime to realize its full value. The Empire State Building was built in a year. I imagine you could produce a stealth bomber, a Ferrari or even a castle in nine months—certainly, an Apple, a Compaq, a Del, or other fruit bearing trees of knowledge. Take a bite. We have become the creators—a few chosen gods.

Gods and generals, scientists and inventors, and I stop. Look at all the breakthroughs: the inventions, the technological advancements, and the wars. Then look at the gods, the generals and the creators. And, certainly, the creators need re-creators to sweat in their shops. But the creators' sweatshops are different. In a reverse paradox, they pay to sweat at places with names like Curves, Gold's, and LA Fitness. Placing the products; yeah, you say you want a revolution.

The Beatles sang of revolution. And I imagine these revolutionaries knew the power of music, the power of the message, the power of English, as they invaded America. And side-by-side we now fight, but then, in the 1960s, there was another Civil War, in a place called Vietnam, an appendage to China, a land of re-creators—

American Perversity
Sex, Politics and Religion

the last vestige of a geo-political world, transitioning to a geo-economic one.

The song *Taps* has its origins in the Civil War: Brothers against brothers: Brothers in arms, arms without brothers, brothers without arms. I doubt that very few Americans know the actual origin of *Taps*. It is the lone bugle dirge sounded at most military funerals. It is distinctively American, distinctly powerful, and eerily enigmatic.

The story goes that Capt. Robert Ellicombe was with his men in Virginia—his Union men—near Harrison's landing. Across a small strip of field were the Confederates. In a lull in the battle, in the night, the captain heard moaning, dying, cries, and so he crawled out to see if he could comfort the dying man. Just like a father would. And Ellicombe, the Union captain, moving across the deadly playing field, found his own son, a player on the other team, now a Confederate soldier who had been studying music in the South and had enlisted in the Confederate Army without telling his father.

Ellicombe tried to have a full military status funeral, but because of his son's "enemy" status he was only partially granted his request. He asked a lone musician, a bugler, to play the notes to a group of musical notes he had found in his dead son's pocket.

> Day is done, gone the Sun,
> From the lakes, from the hills, from the sky;
> All is well, safely rest, god is nigh.
> Fading light, dims the sight,
> And a star, gems the sky, gleaming bright,
> From afar, drawing nigh, falls the night.
> Thanks and praise, four our days,
> 'Neath the sun, 'neath the stars 'neath the sky;
> As we go, this we know, God is nigh ...

That is the *Taps Story*. It is a song of family, of life, of death.

Michael Jordan's father—like Bill Cosby's son—each died by the bullet, but not in Dodge. No, one was in a Lexus, the other in a Mercedes, created by creators, recreated by invaders. What's that bulge? Tora, tora, tora... The invasion of the Germans and the Asians had begun—the axis of autos, winners and losers.

William Bradford Borden

Michael Jordan and Michael Jackson are each in the political section; so, I will attempt to be as incorrectly correct as I can be. You can correct my incorrectness by pointing out my observations. I don't claim to be correct or political—or, for that matter, even remotely calm, cool or collected. I am trying to collect myself and think where I'm going with this chapter of Michaels, of majesty, of kings. Political it shall be, that is sure—representing America, the state of the Union.

What do I think of America? I write of America, right in America, and I feel a part of America, and American apart—united and divided.

The pen I now write with was the gift a student, a black American woman—Ericka, who is married to an African man. And she gave me this pen, which I treasure, as I scribe—a gift of kindness, appreciation and thanks. And I thank Ericka for her words, on a paper with a rose and at the top, in bold, it reads, "Thank you Professor Borden," and it is written like poetry in form, with the lines centered, going down:

> I thank you for every attempt to keep your/students
> interested in your class. /I thank you for listening to us
> as a whole. /I thank you for not giving me the funny
> look/every time I came late to class. /I know I could
> have done better in your class, /but time was not on my
> side. Thank you. Your student, Ericka

Two years before, I was given as a gift a book by a black male student, a gift if you will, along with an accompanying note. The book, *Breaking the Chains of Psychological Slavery* by Na'Im Akbar, Ph.D., was the gift of "Najik." I'll have to check my old roll book, because he wrote me a letter but didn't sign his name.

The tone is certainly different from Ericka's. You might call it militant. Aren't we all? Don't we fight for what is right in America? His letter doesn't begin like Ericka's with "Thank you Professor Borden," but instead with, "Retort to Borden." Typed in black and white, machine-driven, computer-generated, it begins:

American Perversity
Sex, Politics and Religion

Based upon the ridiculous diatribe I was subjected to yesterday, concerning my black experience. I was compelled to write this retort to quell your ever-revolving racism. Because the world has whipped me so, I've become misery's child.

Much of this seems like a direct excerpt from *Raisin in the Sun*, but I will continue, copying "his" words.

But before I do, it is with words that we can create domains, leave our marks, and mark our territory. And the alpha male dog, in a white house, scruffy but brilliant, aggressive but passive, was desperately in need of attention. And they called the dog Clint, after the country star, Clint Black, a melodious, country professional. The president was Southern (big surprise, right? The Southern president listened to Clint Black, the namesake of the dog, scruffy little Clint—the dog that was.) One day, the chief of staff—who seemed to have a handle on things—was pressed by the secretary, pressed to the climactic question of, "Why is Clint on the dress?" "Why is he on the dress?" the press secretary repeated, and the chief of staff, putting his thinking cap on his head, and then using it—his head—responded, "Why is Clint on anything? Why is Clint on everything? Why isn't Clint on Santa Monica?"

That dog had free will I am certain. Why not call Clint Will? Certainly, it is, to risk the use of a cliché, a "dog-eat-dog world." I wonder what kind of food, what kind of treats and desserts Clint would like. What kind of diet is Clint on?

"Retort to Borden," continues:

"Have you cried for me? For what I go through? No! The next time you choose to measure a people, measure them right." (My note; read *Raisin in the Sun*.) "That means take into account the hills and valleys they've crossed to get to where they are."

This should be double or even triple quoted. Great words, but...words are sometimes all we have. The "retort" continues, but the copying is laborious, someone else's words. The lifting of ideas seems more acceptable, but not the words, not the letters, not the power.

The copied words continue:

67

William Bradford Borden

"I have every right to be angry about the never ending plight of my people…"

Things obviously mattered to" "—especially evident in some of his more original word selections as he continued:

"I realize my anger wisely and that is the reason it has been given to you in the form of poetry and essays. My anger and pain is not unfounded. It is based upon the continued subjugation of people of color. You need to stop presenting yourself as the great white hope who needs to tame the uncivilized savages. Remember, people of color are civilization. Obviously, you need some lessons on history and race relations."

Martin Luther King, who had his own serious accusations of plagiarism, would be proud of "Najik" as am I, hearing his voice, now in his words.

Like Oprah, Michael Jordan was born under the sign of Aquarius—he on Feb. 17, 1963, an Aquarian, in the Age of Aquarius. And had it dawned on people how Jordan got air? The heir apparent, another king was to come. This one was born in the North, a true Yankee, Jordan, of the Empire State—Brooklyn, Baby. The family headed south soon after—a reverse commute, ancestral homelands, tillers of America, people of soul …

"Retort to Borden" continues:

> If you choose to discuss my blackness in class, please give me the opportunity to answer. I welcome a lively, productive debate because it affords me the chance to school you. You know, give you some things to think about. Never, ever should you equate those three butt kickings you received with my bouts against the mighty beast of white power that hovers over this land like dense fog. It's insulting. Hell, it is down right racist. Of course you shouldn't be angry anymore, but then again you are since you brought them up in the discussion.

American Perversity
Sex, Politics and Religion

His words are powerful, but I must say that in all of my black/white conflicts, none of the "bouts" was ever one-on-one—always attacked, group aggression, rage in the machine.

There is a wonderful essay by Zora Neale Hurston, called *How it Feels to be Colored Me* "Najik" probably read it in class, and it talks about moving on, not planted in the past, no longer victims. The retort finishes and it exhausts me—the copying. Duplicating, like a sequestered monk...empty:

> My anger is a necessary emotion and the crisis of your racism strikes at the heart and soul of my being. Guess what? I'm not buying the death you're selling. I come to be educated, not ridiculed for feeling angry about my black experience. I have enclosed the book for you to open a new chapter in your book of life. It will explain a whole lot about the racist ideologies that still persist to this day.

The book about "psychological slavery" has a black-and-white picture of the author on the back and it says he's been a guest on *Oprah*. I wonder if I'll be invited. I wonder if I'd go.

"Najik" finishes, perhaps breaking some chains of his perceived slavery—I am no psychologist—and kindly he warns: "Be careful though, because you may become smart after this homemade education." An allusion to the Malcolm X essay, *A Homemade Education*, which I'm sure we read in class. He continues: "You probably don't know you're racist, but get a mirror and you can't help but see the racist you thought you weren't but the one you've come to be."

I want to shout to "Najik" "Stop looking in the mirror! Look at me, let's talk." How appropriate that, in the air, Marvin Gaye sings about war not being the answer. And the Gaye man was also shot. Shot by another Gaye, his father, in Los Angeles, *The City of Angels,* and the magical Marvin continues to ask, "What's going on?" and I want to ask the same thing. Those are just a couple of perspectives—all in black and white.

69

William Bradford Borden

Black to white is something Michael Jackson could probably relate to on several not so ephemeral surfaces. The "transformation" began in Gary, Ind., on Aug. 29, 1958. Michael Jackson would be the seventh of nine children. Jackson might then feel in seventh heaven with children. And, for some reason, I think of the seven deadly sins: lust, envy, pride, anger, sloth, greed, and...the seventh—I can't remember. How deadly.

In 1979, the year I graduated high school, Michael Jackson was 21 and had been performing since he was five. Remember when the pug-nosed, dark-brown, Afro-headed kid let the world know. Maybe you've seen the video. He told us; he sang to us; the angel sang telling us he would be there. A child then, and in 1979, at 21, perhaps always a child, the consummate Peter Pan released *Off the Wall* which was the first album to ever spawn four number one hit songs.

Numbers, yet so impressive: the seventh child, the seven deadly sins—touching all of us—seventh heaven, and the house would be full, walls complete, with another seven, which would come in the form of a thriller not in Manila, but in the album. *Thriller* would become, in 1982, the world's largest selling album of all time, selling more than 51 million copies. It also broke the record of four with seven number one singles...

Michael Jordan, on the other hand hit a few singles himself. In 1975, four years before Jackson was going to start bouncing us off the walls, Jordan was down in North Carolina playing ball. Born in Brooklyn, the "Yankee free agent" returned to his farm team. In 1975, at the age of 12, the Dixie Youth Association named Jordan "Mr. Baseball," where he played pitcher and shortstop on a Little League team.

Numbers and statistics I report to you and I feel like an uncertified public accountant. Life—maybe much more so in America than anywhere in the world—is often boiled down to statistics and demographic—basic math, if you will. If numbers then are the basis of what we do, then what are we built on? Quite possibly on geometric foundations of right and wrong angles, and again I assert that one can write, to right that which is wrong, some in song, some in the air, and some with prayer.

American Perversity
Sex, Politics and Religion

What prayers were said at Michael Jordan's father's funeral? Perhaps, the 23rd Psalm, the one I read at my own father's funeral... "Yea, through I walk through the valley of the shadow of death..." And even the holy books are numbered, OT and NT, east and west, old and new; and one of the books of the old is even called *Numbers*... Relative? Yes. Relevant? Maybe. Related to anything? Perhaps.

I must—at least for your sake, and maybe for heavens, because our days our numbered—try to relate this to something—to politics, to people, to black power.

In a 2003 *Newsweek* cover article, they ran a piece dealing with black power, but it dealt with the black power of women. The power of the matriarch, so prevalent in the black community, powerful women raising powerful children, the father often absent, statistics and demographics, numbers...

Jordan's and Jackson's fathers were both very much in their lives—first in their mothers' lives, fruits of their loins, algebraic equations of x-and y-chromosomes. The product of the equation in each case: a Michael, the name of the archangel. And weren't there arcs in geometry, and arcs of a ball in the air, and arcs of careers? Arks and covenants... Two by two they got on the ark, animals of all kinds, starting all over. The days of the journey were numbered to 40—days and night, light and dark.

Numbered days, and today is the 24th day of April 2003, and there are many who say that when the final day comes—the one to the right of the hyphen—that their numbers have come up. It almost seems like a game of chance, of bingo, the lotto. And when is that final number selected? Has it already been written or is it possible to sink one more, not getting caught in the net—swoosh—right at the buzzer? And the buzzards are left hanging; the game has gone into overtime. There's another chance to play, to win and lose. Certainly the final score will be more. What are the odds? I guess the odds are even that the score will be odd. Or even, if you're odd; even then, there are only 10 and 10 isn't one, which is one with a zero. Zero, the first number; and zero through nine equals 10. Five odd and five even... odd, that what we have is a rather even-handed handful.

William Bradford Borden

A handful of dirt is such a graphic transition. Ashes to ashes, dust to dust, and even though this transition from paragraph to paragraph, from idea to idea, is not smooth, "What is?" I question. Transition is inevitable. Transition is timeless in the cycle of days. A year has 365, almost like a circle with its 360, but with five more for good luck. Five extra chips thrown in for a little more play, 5 extra days, and 120 more hours to start the circle again. 'Round and 'round we go. And when we get around to looking at our radius, our diameter, our shape, and then functioning in all the variables—working on the solution—it makes me wonder, in this "circle of life," if we ever really get to the core.

And the drill instructors bellowed, "One, two, three four," and the Marines, part of another corps, responded, "One, two, three four, United States Marine Corps." Getting the numbers right, the number left of the hyphen, written in stone—already etched.

To the right of Michael Jordan's father's stone is a final tally, a final score, game over. The number reads, and isn't that an interesting concept that we read numbers? You might think we need to number words more. Add them up. I wonder how much a Lexus—which is basically a Toyota with a different name, a different dollar sign, a different status—how much a top-of-the-line Lexus would have cost in 1993. You wouldn't think someone's life. Day by day, rotating around the circle, seemingly infinite, but everything must be counted. That is one thing you can most certainly count on.

On July 23, 1993, James Jordan was murdered in his fancy Lexus automobile, much like Bill Cosby's son, who was murdered for his luxury Mercedes. One headline could have read, "America's son loses his father" and the other, "America's father loses his son." One in Carolina, one in California—east coast/west coast—one in a Japanese, the other in a German. Dollar signs in the eyes of the auditors: preferring Benjamin to Jackson, keeping up with the Jones', and getting air with the Jordan's. Wanting a piece of the pie, but not quite satisfied—wanting more and more, gross gluttons. How perverse.

There are many pieces of the pie, and because of the sheer numbers there are a lot more poor whites, "white trash" often their label, and it is a group I rarely encounter. Yet, here they are again,

72

American Perversity
Sex, Politics and Religion

the large white, wheel-chaired woman with two blonde girls—the Depression, dustbowl era, black-and-white-photo-looking one. The one who I had chased down the street a week or so before and given her a 10. And I now know her name, because the man who must be "David" pushes her, limping a little, with a leg brace over his black jeans. And David has a similar tattoo, with a different name on the same place on the side of his neck. "Michelle" it reads. Michelle and David, trash to some, background players to others. Does anyone take them out? And out they go, like the trash that the Starbucks pusher had pushed out before, on a dolly.

Hello, as model enters as white trash exits. The model now leans over the counter to sign her name, so tall that the bend creates a near 90-degree angle, and I would love to measure that, yeah, "measure that good." Yes, and I think back to what someone had said to the walrus-looking guy in a uniform, pushing the grinds out the door, what she had said, about nothing being more attractive than a man with the trash. I wonder what she thinks of David; I wonder what it would be like to take out Michelle? To take out the trash as the model parades by—a fountain of youth, out the same door with the trash. We all have our entrances and our exits. One day at a time...

It is Friday, the 25th of April and the Shabbat, the going down of the sun, beginning the day of rest of the seventh day. I'm fairly certain that the keeping holy of the Sabbath is one of the commandments, one of ten—just a number to sum.

No math metaphors here. Have I begun a paragraph yet with "no"? I'm just trying to get into the groove, not necessarily be groovy, and it is difficult to feel groovy, cool or hip when you're doing the numbers; but, then again, it's all a matter of perspective and relevance.

Mr. Terrell made math and numbers, not to mention kindness, high school and teaching relevant; and for the final pages of this chapter, I think I'll shift from Jackson and Jordan to another black man whom I had the honor to call teacher, Mr. Terrell, who taught me to love math, in particular Algebra (and Islam and the Arab world must be praised for the great contributions to numbers and math, and, also to the preservation of ours). I still remember the power of the FOIL method in solving algebraic equations. Interesting that the foil,

William Bradford Borden

or fool, in drama is often tasked with helping to solve and resolve conflict by holding up a mirror and saying, "Look!" One thing is most certain—Mr. Terrell was no fool.

Many things in my life have blessed me and sometimes I haven't appreciated my blessings. Sometimes I haven't even realized them until years later.

Starting with Miss Jones in the first grade, when the love of reading set me on fire and so did she with her soul sister ways. She was calm, hip and confident in a '60s way, the emerging power of women—black power women.

Five years later, in sixth grade, I got my first black mother, the eternal Mrs. Young. She had beautiful graying hair, a fountain of wisdom, and a divine soul. She also helped guide me into my teens.

Three years later, in ninth grade, I walked into Mr. Terrell's class, to a true soul brother, master of mathematics, Algebra One with Mr. Terrell. I knew it would be interesting—he with the timeless face of kindness, the laughter of a saint, and big Afro-pick. Mr. Terrell knew the power of one, the power of now—black power.

Much of my balance—and I have begun to find it—I owe to my trilogy of teachers, Jones, Young and Terrell. The power of yin and yang is the power of the black and white. Thank you, you three, for teaching me the beauty of meeting the black and white, for finding that balance in the gray area, the power of education, the power of people, black people, black power, my masters, master teachers— harvesters for America.

Just a bit on the power of numbers and much of that power is now bit on computer bytes, and right there is the force multiplier. Think computers and numbers and Bill Gates and his wealth. All measured in numbers, like the music that beats, different numbers in time, depending on the numbered station; or the digital, numeric CD, playing a numbered song; to the cost of that car that carries your sound system; to your height, your weight, your shoe size; to all your measurements; to the number on your license, to the date the same is written; to the page of this book; to the stars in the sky.

Yes, to the very fabric of your existence, numbers in letters, DNA. And today is a number and yesterday, too; and there are three words that have that sound but different meanings and spelling, too (and that

American Perversity
Sex, Politics and Religion

is one, "too"), and the other two (that is another), and to (that is the third) continue this equation could go on ad infinitum...

The equation has changed as the demographics and the location as well. Old people ride on "Old Town Trolley Tours." Gone south, L.A. to San Diego, different players and pushers, trying to make a buck in Paradise and I question, is the paradise lost or forgotten, and who forgets as the sunrise on America begins to set?

Yes, the sunrise of the "greatest generation"—those who fought and served in WWII—begins to fade, begins to end. And as they pass by in the trolley, on a tour to a place many had saved all their lives to come and see; and paradise is witnessed, but the vision is clouded, the dream unsure. But, as the passengers on "The Old Town Trolley" peer down from their wheeled trolley, they see the witness to the "American Dream." Americans, walk by, playing their parts, "California dreaming." And maybe the greatest, heading toward sunset, see that their vision had come to fruition and the knowledge that the tree was still blooming was comforting in their retirement.

In Franklin today, the quote is from Ayn Rand, the writer of the fantastic novel *The Fountainhead*, and I thank dear Anna for that gift, and the quote is so appropriate. "Happiness" is the theme, and, I often ask people what makes them happy, or rather, what the key to happiness is. In *The Art of Happiness*, the Dalai Lama asserts that the key to happiness is to give love. Don't worry about receiving it in return, just give love, and it—the love—will bring happiness. Ayn Rand's words relate to values and I like that, and she writes, "Happiness is that state of consciousness which proceeds from the achievement of one's values."

When one of my students asked what I valued—you may remember—I responded, after a thought, "love." I also so value education, and it is through teaching that I can accomplish, or hope to contribute and maybe even make a difference, one way or another, preferably positive, to people like Ericka, and Najik, and also people like Shoshana. Because, people like Miss Jones, Mrs. Young and Mr. Terrell made that kind of difference for me. Good people, black people, American people.

Shoshana is the daughter of a famous singer from a very famous '60s "girl" band. I had the pleasure to meet the lovely mother at a

William Bradford Borden

back-to-school night, and I was so proud to be Shoshana's teacher—just for a moment of time—and then it was time to graduate high school myself and move on to college. You may also remember that I bought a yearbook that last year of high school in Los Angeles, in 2000, and the students signed it and Shoshana wrote to me, her teacher. Teaching me, she wrote:

"Hey (6/19) Mr. Borden. What's up? How's it going? Even though I've only spent one year with you, it's been really fun. I wish you could stay, and I'm sure a lot of people feel the same way because you're such a good and fun teacher. I probably would have never gotten through 4th Honors Class with those kids yelling and screaming all the time.

You may not think that you make a difference in some of your student's lives but you do. With your attitude and being so open and honest with your students, they feel they can do the same with you. Like so many people in the beginning of the year couldn't speak in front of anybody, they were so shy. Now they're running for prom queen and going on tour and stuff like that.

I bet you're wondering "who" that person is, huh? Well, it was me, yes, I used to be shy, but I got used to going in front of the class and speaking. I wish you wouldn't go so I could get to know you more and see what an even better teacher you are. But since you're leaving, I have to say my good-byes and move on because somebody else is waiting in line to sign your yearbook. But, anyways, goodbye Mr. Borden and I hope you come back to visit our graduating year "2003." We'll miss you!!! Shoshana."

I miss you, Miss Shoshana, Miss America. Thank you for bridging the gap: black and white, East Coast and West, student and teacher. And so, with a touch of soul, for my soul has been touched and with respect I thank you—and Jordan and Jackson as well. Yes "Najik" you may have thought you schooled me in your "Retort to Borden," but I think I schooled you too. It has been an honor to teach, to school and "be schooled"—old school and new.

6
Horticulture

Bush begins Chapter Six, a pivotal chapter, a pivotal president, a pivotal time—the first presidency of the 21st century. Just the sound, "the 21st century" has a powerful ring, and bells toll as alarms are sounded and the sound is charming—like a snake, slithering, sliding, slippery, a bit of onomatopoeia, being true to the sounds, the rhythms, the cheers. Saluting America in the 21st century... Blackjack!

Bush does not seem like a gambler and that is probably good; but, that is probably not a good sentence—certainly one must take the chances and George Walker Bush, a k a "W," and I realize that I started the paragraph with Bush, and also the first one—two Bushes in a row, metaphorically forming a hedge, protecting America, standing tall.

In the role of President, Bush is also commander in chief. I need to figure out how I will address him to differentiate him from his father. I think I will respectfully call him "W," which happens to be the 23rd letter of the English alphabet, which we get from the English; God Save the Queen, and God bless Great Britain. I like how Bush usually ends with "God Bless America," and America has been blessed.

The root of "W," "W's" roots ... "W" is 23 in the English letter scheme, and he is the 43rd president. He is the first right-handed president since Reagan. Bush's father (who took the handoff from the lefty "The Gipper" Reagan), was a lefty who handed it to another

77

William Bradford Borden

lefty, "Wild Bill" Clinton, a cowboy in his own right, but he wasn't really that much of a lefty, so he handed back to the right, to another Bush. Left, right, left...

And I see that Hillary got an $8 million book advance—I sure hope it's good. I wonder if she had any interns help her with the process. I wonder how Hillary conjugates the verb "to be." I wonder what her definition of "is," is. I also wonder if Hillary is irritated by Bush; her husband seemed to be, but then again I think Clinton really likes Bush, maybe just not quite as much as Hillary. I think Bush has really grown on her.

Waxing poetic I am not. I have never waxed. Madame Tussaud has waxed both Clinton and Bush. I imagine Clinton would enjoy being waxed by the Madame. I wonder if Hillary's been waxed. I hope you will forgive the wordplay. I imagine if I had an $8 million advance like "Health Care Hilary," I would be more reverent. But, then again I don't feel she and her husband were very reverent or moral people. I highly recommend the book *Dereliction of Duty* for an insight as to how debauched things really were.

I have heard, and read, and seen many things in my life and I understand my irreverence toward Clinton. I am saddened at my words but not apologetic, for I feel as though he was disgraceful toward the office of the White House, the office of president, and figurehead of America.

Each word I choose, "figurehead" for example, has potential ramifications in regard to this discourse, and the words come in turn, in turn—yes in turn they come—and come, and come, like a spot on a dress. See Spot run, run Spot, run.

Dick replaces Tarzan. It's hard to replace Dick. Dick and Jane, seeing Spot run. Now Dick is calling to Spot, "Come, Spot, come," and Spot is coming and, in turn, so is Jane, and their names have been changed to protect the relevance of a story—most certainly not the greatest story ever told, but a timeless story of planting and harvesting, a story of fruits and roots.

The image of two proud, solid Bushes on either side of a promising, strapping tree is a sad one, a tragic one, and an unfortunate one. In fact, in many respects it is a story of a tree much like the *Giving Tree*, where, in this case, the tree mutilates itself in the

78

American Perversity
Sex, Politics and Religion

apparent pursuit of feeding on forbidden fruit, not the kind found in Santa Monica, but instead the kind found in a murky pond, with the purple-grey hue of oil run-off, and the sun creating a mirror effect.

The protagonist looks in, and like Narcissus, falls in love with his image. And, on the banks of the trailer park, the tree's roots reach for the oily pond, full of Texas crude, but this is Arkansas and the roots seek sustenance in the wrong place. And it is so unfortunate because the tree could have been a redwood, a sequoia—grand and glorious.

So Dave and crew, feed the trunk and branches into the chopping machine behind the green truck. But the roots lie below, feeling lost and without direction as the bushes continue to grow around the foot-level stump of what could have been. "Who's protecting the forests?" you might ask. "Not the bushes," you might respond, but then again bushes seem to know their roots, and the root to oil—Texas crude— and see how rude I have been?

In Italian, the word for rude is "maleducato," which simply means badly educated, and that is the sadness, or rather irony, of the rude— the fact that those that are rude are often unaware, and the simple fact is that rude people are often those who have been badly educated and, hence, there is not a strong root structure.

A strong sense of structure was seemingly lacking in the Clinton White House and is apparently now present in the Bush White House. There seems to be a much stronger sense of mission, protocol, and decorum in the first of the 21st century White House. And for all of Clinton's reaching out to African Americans, "W" has been equally, if not more adept, at bridging the gap—think Dr. Condoleezza Rice and Gen. Colin Powell.

Because this is the "W" chapter, not the Clinton one, I shall move on, and I am reminded of a joke my 8-year-old niece—a true California kid with a heart of gold—told me. She asked, "How come, when there were two morons, a big moron and a little moron, the little moron was able to hang on longer?" And the reason was, "The little moron was a little more on."

Moronic, right? Left, right, left... What is left? What is right? What is wrong? Is it wrong to question? To be or not to be, that is the question. What about questioning authority? That seemed to be a declaration during the '60s—"Question authority"—and I find it

79

William Bradford Borden

interesting that the root—and we have come somewhat full circle—the root of authority is "author." "Makhtub"—it is written, and my students who read *The Alchemist* will remember that. But do we question authors? Do you question me? I hope so. I often question myself. Maybe the pen is mightier than the sword.

My notes now are letters, the 26 of the English alphabet, and I pen these words and try to make music, try to make sense, not sure of the genre, not sure that it matters. What does matter? Are a man's accomplishments genuinely gauged, or is it in the gauging itself, be it 12-gauge or 20-gauge shot, 8mm or 35mm film, 10W40 or 10W50 oil? Yes, how do we gauge and how do we engage? Is it really all that matters—the notes, the letters—or it is rather their arrangement, juxtaposition and composition that measure the man?

Scales are often how people, places, and things are measured and so, in deference to my current commander in chief, I will try to present an equal and spirited defense. Defense is what I played in soccer, left full back, and it is difficult to score from the defense. Why do we have a Department of Defense, but not a Department of Offense? Would that be offensive? In sports, the old adage is often that a good defense is the best offense. Usually, I believe, it is said that more offensively, in the context of the best offense is a good defense, but please, don't hold me to that because I could be wrong and then I might require a really good defense attorney. The prosecutors in the O.J. Simpson trial, Marcia Clark and Chris Darden, I understand may have been seeing if the glove fit outside of the courtroom. But that could be pure speculation. Could I be prosecuted for speculating simply because I'm rushing for the gold offensively? I must say in my defense that I wouldn't want to offend.

Back to the question now, which is, if there are defense attorneys, aren't prosecutors essentially offense attorneys? O.J. the athlete, the Juice, knew about offense, the weakness of defenders, and running through the middle. Certainly, he also knew the power of dream work, the power of teamwork—visions of a dream team, the trial of the century, a brilliant game, and a spirited defense.

You almost had to give them a hand, with or without glove; the dream team won the game. But, the tragic irony and sadness was that the fans felt no euphoria. Some from O.J.'s team maybe—yes, maybe

American Perversity
Sex, Politics and Religion

them—but the true fans, the true aficionados, the true lovers of the game—the lovers of family, of virtues, of love—they felt no satisfaction. Because even though they were sports fans and may have known the wonder of Orenthal J. Simpson on the field and in the game; still others—other true fans—had seen the O.J. on screen and he was good and funny.

I smile when I think of *The Naked Gun* and O.J.'s lovely smile, but now my one smile goes away. I feel it and the pen is harder on the paper. Elton John sings that, "Butterflies are free to fly," and my smile is gone as I think of Nicole and Ron, and how maybe they were in a game they didn't know they were playing. Or maybe they thought they were playing another game with another set of rules, and different equipment—glasses instead of gloves.

It is interesting, maybe, that the players with glasses were perhaps seeing each other when the lone player, with gloves that fit, ran right up the middle—a running back, breaking up the tango. And it took two to tango, he had always been told, but he wasn't always sure about that. And as he packed his suitcase, off to another game, the player watched *Three's Company*, and perhaps he remembered former threesomes, but now preferred foursomes, for golf had become his game. He needed a set of rules to conform, but like the fans—the true fans—he felt cheated because he knew he hadn't played fairly—that his coaches had cheated, and that the record didn't really count.

What does count? Do you? Certainly. And again I have broken the fourth wall and come into the audience. Thank you for welcoming me into your mind; thank you for your time; and I am stuck with what to write. I am a very confident (and my mother wrote "arrogant" in a graduation letter I shared in Chapter Three). Yes, I am very confident, but I hope not overly and ... enough of me. I do believe in humility, and I am touched and honored if you read my words. It is so very humbling.

I could never write a self-help book. I often feel like I can't even help myself, but being in the moment is momentous for me and I realize that it comes not only in writing, but also in teaching. And I realize how fortunate I am, as I remember how, today my college English class, respectful and proud, surprised me with a cake and cards, gifts and appreciation.

81

William Bradford Borden

And I appreciate my students—Californians, Americans and guests. Lots of guests... Some are here for a long journey and others quite possibly never to return. And they tell me their stories and I tell them mine. Stories of the Philippines, Iran and Vietnam, stories of Iraq and Afghanistan, Korea and Pakistan, Japan and Amsterdam, Thailand and Greece, Mexico and El Salvador, Guatemala and Chile.

I want to stop and say I'm surprised that the Latin American countries came so late in my list, and it was just as they came, but maybe because they've been here longer. They seem more settled their journey not so far; the Latinos were here before most. And their roots are in this land with their mestizo souls and blood.

It's interesting that "soul" has a plural. Are they numbered? You might figure. And an interesting juxtaposition: the Latin with the African American. One group came, and comes, willingly; their roots are here, seeds of their forefathers.

The other came from a distant continent, the continent that brought us O.J. and Oprah, Jackson and Jordan, the African continent. Africa, with its wonder and mystery... These people like Leslie, who I'm so proud to call my student, and whose mother died having a botched abortion. She would be so proud of Leslie, her African American daughter, but also cry that it was a forced journey of her people—pulled up from their roots, from the wonder of Africa, the mystery and music of the Dark Continent, a forced journey to the Promised Land, full of milk and honey. "But, what is wrong with gazelles and giraffes?" many of Africa thought. Their roots were still there, but it was a distant land, and their forced journey was certainly no vacation, but what a blessing to America.

A blessing to America and Americans... North, Central, and South; Anglo and Latino, African, Filipino, Persian, Vietnamese, Iraqi and Afghani, Korean and Pakistani, Japanese and Thai, Greek and Mexican, Salvadorian, Chilean, and I realize I forgot China and Israel. And I am blessed, and America is blessed to have these people and to prove something to Rodney King. This other King, the one who help start the L.A. riots. One who could be reading this from a prison. How tragic, to be in the zoo, caged, remembering the roots and what would have been, but like many fools, there is wisdom and his question is, "Can't we all just get along?" And my answer is yes.

American Perversity
Sex, Politics and Religion

I see it in my class, in California, in America. I think maybe we could if we knew the game, and maybe if we played by the old Golden Rule, instead of the new, and who knew? Who are you? Are you a player? I would think yes, as William Shakespeare said "All the men and women merely players." So what's the game, what's your position and—most importantly do you honestly believe that the best defense is a good offense?

What is the game and is it worth playing? Check your schedule, check your equipment and let the games begin. And in the beginning there was… Yes, in the beginning, there was what? I'm not sure. Somewhere I read it was written. Isn't that why we write? To be read? It is a gift that is so very unique—the ability to communicate through the written word. And there are those scales of justice, trying to find balance, to find the perfect part in the best script you can find. Maybe you should write your own! Makhtub!

Shabbat Shalom. It is Friday evening, the second of May 2003, and the time is 20:32, twenty thirty-two (twenty minus twelve equaling eight for the hour; the minutes stay the same. 8:32 p.m.), simple math, numbers, addition and subtraction. More than 24 hours have passed since my writing time yesterday, and I find it ironic that people often say when somebody dies that they "passed away." Does that mean they passed the class? Perhaps they were only auditing or perhaps they believed in re-incarnation and they were the teacher, having learned the material many courses past.

How are your courses? Are they interesting? Of course, your courses are personal. The people talk, caffeine pushers chat, and Elton sings and the words mix with mine and it seems written, and it is—literally—next to my left shoulder. The new, freestanding placard replaces the one for Italian coffee. Now I am encouraged to: "Explore our African coffees this summer." (I am further advised, in their own parenthetical aside, right next to mine—literally—to the right… right now) ("No passport needed.")

For Shabbat, a passport is never required, just a desire to connect with the chosen, with the 12 tribes, with a touch of the divine, completing the cycle of a seven-day week. What other things are seven? Mickey Mantle's number; the muses, daughters of Zeus (either seven or nine depending on your sources) and the muses are

83

William Bradford Borden

the roots of music and amusement, the power of women; there is 7th Heaven; the Seven Deadly Sins; the Seven Heavenly Virtues; the seven letters, or tiles, each person plays with in Scrabble; the seven letters of William—yes, Will I am; anything else that is seven? How about the seven-year itch? Have you been scratching? What about dog years? One of ours for seven of theirs...

I find it fascinating that so many things—apparently important, or quite possibly not—require specific and measurable numbers, and "specific" is the operative word. Just look at sports, which are often a metaphor for life, and the concept of teams with rules, players and numbers: baseball with nine; basketball with five; football and soccer with eleven; tennis—singles with two, doubles with four; marathons with thousands; war with thousands more ...numbers for the teams, then numbers for the scores, on and off the court—winners and losers, taking no prisoners.

And so the wordplay continues. Playing against the clock, trying to make a point and it seems like reaching the goal and getting to the subject is not simple, the objective of "W"; and yes, I have previously made that point, and that I beat around things. A connection then with "W" is his connection with education, and how he was reading to schoolchildren when someone called 911. And I wondered the other day, as I looked at the bold sign, large red letters, but not really letters (the letters were in the fine print with some message of warning) these were numbers, posted on the gate, and it advised, "In emergency, call for help," and I realized, as I'm sure many of us had, that the warning had been written long before: 911.

Once again, numbers with profound significance. But the game wasn't as fun as it used to be. And would the numbers be as significant if an amateur found them? Where would that rank? Yes, 911; the two "ones" stood side-by-side like towers, twins, but separated. And the significance of nine... And the first four letters of "significance" giving us "sign," and these were signs of the times; these were New York times. And it was no "cat's meow" and I knew before I wrote that I would not like that reference. But there is more time, especially in the moment, and maybe like the cat, the feline, the lion that sleeps the majority of the day—maybe there is truth in nine lives, but many more than nine were lost.

American Perversity
Sex, Politics and Religion

It was past time, but not America's pastime, which had always been considered baseball, and nine were needed to play, and the towers had been built and the players came. Professionals and amateurs, Muslims and Jews, black and white, men and women, rich and poor, smart and stupid, strong and weak, happy and sad, faithful and empty, young and old, hot and cold—players from the world over, looking for their own towering achievements, building castles in the sky, but the game was over—the score written long before—their jerseys retired, hanging in the heaven. The final score was nine, eleven.

There is some factor—an equation, if you will—that is something to the effect that for every 15 minutes of planning, an hour is saved—a 4 to 1 ratio of accomplishing and achieving goals. Today my Franklin Planner has a quote from Erica Jong, who wrote the novel *Fear of Flying*, and conceptualized the idea of the "zipless fuck" or the "fearless fuck" some kind of fuck—in the air, or a plane, getting that extra mileage in the mile-high club.

I wonder if astronauts are "fucking out of this world"; and I can't help but think (but apologize because of the irreverence), but the song reverberates, the song about Sally riding, and I am reminded of my student, a Cohen (and of the 12 tribes of Israel, the Cohens are the priests). And he told me that the Israeli astronaut that was killed in the shuttle, that it was written in the Torah, the fate of that crew. I believed him.

It didn't surprise me that it all came apart over Palestine. It so often had, but this Palestine was over Texas. It was almost as though a master Global Position Satellite had chosen the place, the exact location, like a laser-guided bunker buster (it was no job for a MOAB. Those mothers seemed to only work well in Florida.) And things were busting up all over in Palestine.

I wonder if Pvt. Jessica Lynch, the one that was "saved" in Iraq, had been saved before. I would imagine so; the people of Palestine, West Virginia, seem pretty religiously fervent. Palestinians usually are.

You see, I am making connections with #43, "W," who I believe is a Methodist, and I would hope, and hope is often all we have. I do try, and even though I grew up an Episcopalian, I prefer spirituality to

William Bradford Borden

religion; I do hope and pray that there is a method to my madness. Maddening, isn't it? That depends on your definition of what "it" is. Yeah, "what it is?"

What is it? Franklin quotes Jong, and it is May 3, and Franklin's focus for the month is *change*, and the question asks, "What can you change to lead your life forward?" Good question, and to the right, Jong's song, her words, which are written, "The trouble is, if you don't risk anything, you risk even more." Good luck. Throw the dice, play your hand, make a wish...

Now, in this wish, in this dream, in this moment, there is the sound of Hebrew, a sound of ancient people, ancient times, and there is a real beauty to these people of Palestine, for they are not domesticated, they are not caged, they live like the ancients, hunters and gatherers, hunted and hunting, gathered and gathering.

They are proud people, strong people, tribal people, and I want to write "my people," but I am not the messiah, chosen by the chosen. I am just a messenger, and the message is of hope, of timelessness, of love. And it is here and there; it is everywhere ... in Texas, in West Virginia, and yes, in Palestine. It is real. Yes, it is real...

And a woman—past her prime, but primed nonetheless—saunters by wearing navy blue Abercrombie sweatpants, and the message from Abercrombie is to join the team. No sweat, no glory, no victory, just a number on a pair of sweat pants representing an allusion. Just like her fake tits that barely jiggle and are void of milk and honey.

Three cops enter. It is 9:09 a.m. the next day, Cinco de Mayo. All three cops are Hispanic, all three Latino, and all three hunters. And they are now on guard, standing their watch, watching some of their own; players on the opposite team, and there is a fine line— maybe a thin blue one—between the two. I wonder if they ask, "Can we get along?" You wonder if they know how important they are. I am happy the men in blue, who stand their watch, know their sweat and blood and toil is here, in America. It always has been for the mestizos; and aren't we all a bit mixed up? It is good the three sit and talk. With coffee, newspapers and guns they are appreciated more so now than ever.

And now is Cinco de Mayo, and apparently it is not a major holiday in Mexico, but it is for much of Los Angeles. Not to just

American Perversity
Sex, Politics and Religion

drink Tecate, Dos Equis and Tequila, but to lift a glass. "Arriba, Abajo, al dentro, al centro—Salud." Happy Cinco de Mayo, a true gift from Mexico, sent north. Muchas Gracias!

Si, muchas gracias, and how bizarre that just now a gardener was dropped off by a friend in a mini Nissan pickup. That is one of the gardener's job descriptions—"picking" it all up—and the gardener gets out waiting for a bus. (I was going to throw in an allusion to gardening, but it seems so forced, allusive even.) Then the gardener, 60-something with a soul a million times that, gets on the bus, token in hand, no gestures.

The peace officers exit for the hunt. Peace officers? Maybe. But believe me; L.A. knows how to wage war. Maybe that is natural. Everyone appreciates a good fight. (But then again writing, "everyone" is inherently untrue in that nothing is absolute, definitely not, never.) "To protect and serve" on the side of car number 85347 drives west down Ventura, past the Bank of America that was just the scene of a shooting. Yes, it is 5-5, Cinco de Mayo, a perfect ten, "mano a mano," hand to hand, side by side, welcome to Los Angeles, welcome to California, welcome to America ... North, South and Central.

If you build a well, will the people come? Will you come to the well? Well come, you are told, welcome. And here you come; you want to come again and again, but there are many wells to choose from...

Gold is by rule golden—what a powerful word, "rule"—breaking and setting them, and in the process often changing them, and somewhere in the Bible it is written, something to the effect, an admonition if you will, "Judge not lest ye be judged."

Enough of this drama—it is comforting to know what you don't know, or know what you don't want to do, and then spend time doing what you love. Doing what you will remember with fondness in the past, will treasure with passion in the present, and will look forward to in the future. May your life be one of perpetual joy and laughter— not in the vein of hedonism and narcissism, but instead in the artery of the flow of life. Life at the well; and will you? Yes, you will.

So then may you appreciate the uncountable, the timeless, the *Bomwish*...the blood, the oil, the milk and honey, the water, the "I,"

87

William Bradford Borden

the sand, the honey—and the gold. Yes, go for the gold, get in the race; and find a reason to believe (and that is literally on at Starbucks, Rod Stewart is crooning, Scottish Soul. But it is a message to me, and to you. "A reason to believe"…) Yes, a prayer must end, and maybe there is eternal wisdom in "The Lord's Prayer" and maybe a fitting one if you know.

I contemplate, and isn't that part of prayer, contemplating? Not just reading the lines but reflecting on their meanings—the connotations as well as the denotations? And it is the connecting with words, perhaps, that brings us closer to divinity, creating heaven and hell with the stroke of a pen, tap of a key or push of a button.

Life and death in the balance, creators and re-creators, and we should pray for all of them… and the message at the Gap has changed, and now it proclaims "GET SOME COLOR," all in capitals, bold letters insisting. Yes, get some color, GSC at the Gap, and at the end of the day across the gap, the movement from the past to present; there is often a rainbow. You can get you some there, and it is paradise, full of color and hope, and there is gold at the end of the line, for all who have run the race, from the beginning to the end. Gold for all the good players, the actors and the architects—for all who have played fairly, acted nobly and created passionately.

And the prayer came close to the end when the congregation was preparing to go and the Prayer of the Lord began to end "Give us this day…" and I realized that was all we really needed, and I realized that a need is different than a want; and I want you to be happy and fulfilled, full of happiness and laughter, love and music, health and passion. Yes, give us this day, because—quite possibly—tomorrow never comes.

Maybe this is a way to transfer to 43, to "W," the president that is. Taking it back to the all-American; Mr. Brokaw, the midwestern boy done good… "Reporting from Studio City this is Bradford Borden. Back to you Tom…"

"Thank you, Bradford. Bradford Borden…"

"This just in, George Bush's resume… (I would imagine you understand what I am attempting, and so I have broken your fourth wall again and come into your theatre, peeked through your curtain to report what was reported to me by my Shakespeare student Stephanie

American Perversity
Sex, Politics and Religion

who e-mailed me the resume and also gave me my mini *Zohar* which I treasure.)

There are 22 volumes to the *Zohar*, the religious Jewish text with a focus on mysticism, and magic and numbers... and facing east, in my dining area, in two, three-foot tall, neutral wood bookcases that stand side-by-side on the white Roman marble, and there are 11 in each tower, 22 with both, and the numbers move west. Right to left. What is left to write if it's already been written? I guess that all depends on what your definition of "it" is—right? Write right! And now your left...

Your left, right, left, and that's how we do it when our military marches. We begin with the left. Yeah, that's right, we put our left foot in, and then our right foot out; but this ain't no hokey pokey.

To my right is a group of lusty Latinas. They are fine and passionate. There is lots of laughter, lust in their laughter—lusty Latinas and I love them and their zest for life. To my right is a Jewish mother, talking about her school-aged daughter: "...bare legs, wide belt, perfect body, just legs, scaring me, hiding her in a closet, scaring me..."

Does the lust scare the Jewish mother? Does it scare you? If it does, maybe you should ask yourself why, or rather when. And just then, a hard-bodied, 30-something, wearing tight blue sweat pants swooshes by, and on her behind there is a colorful symbol—the symbol of peace. Yes, peace on her firm ass. Who wouldn't want a piece of that? Now she exists, parading by and shaking things up, trying to strike a balance—a balance between lust and love; but, for many, both concepts—the lust and love—had long since evaporated, the well gone dry.

Am I irrigating you? How is your balance? Your love and your lust; do you still seek them out? And out of the soul of the earth we take the timelessness: past, present and future. Well, well, well...are you gushing?

Did you take a dip today? Did you shower and bathe? Was it steamy? And did your ideas and dreams evaporate? Do you remember when there was more lust than love and smile; and wonder how covertly you were advised that one took precedence over the other? One good, one evil; gods and devils, yin and yang... yeah the

William Bradford Borden

love, from the greeting cards had been advised and written. But they also realized that people wanted messages of lust as well, sending messages of lust and intent.

The most likely defense was "don't kill the messenger," and the messenger was just trying to find a balance, delivering bullets and bombs—lust bullets and love bombs. Finding another battle to try and win the war by trying to find balance. Like Dorothy over the rainbow, looking for gold, trying to go home full of lust and love, home to Kansas, and that's whence the messengers came—Kansas, City, that is. And the message from Missouri swept like a tornado going east, sweeping the mess west, then north and south, looking for balance, all in a pile. Laying down plowshares but still hunting and waging. Sword in one hand, pen in the other...

"Back to you, Tom," and I turn it back over, and that is acknowledged. "Thanks Bradford" and now Brokaw is in control, but only for a moment. "When we come back we'll have an in-depth report on Bush's resume. At the break I say to Tom that it looks like—with all the commercials for prescription drugs—the news is being supported and run drug cartels that push their product between the carnage. The line producer gives a five-second warning and then counts down: three, two, one...

George W. Bush

$ Produced a Hollywood slasher B movie

$ Bought an oil company, but couldn't find any oil in Texas. The company went bankrupt shortly after "W" sold stock.

$ Bought the Texas Rangers baseball team in a sweetheart deal that took land using taxpayer money. Biggest move: Traded Sammy Sosa to the Chicago White Sox.

$ With father's help (and his name) was elected Governor of Texas.

Accomplishments as governor:

$ Changed pollution laws for power and oil companies and made Texas the most polluted state in the union.

$ Replaced Los Angeles with Houston as the most smog-ridden city in America. Cut taxes and bankrupted the Texas government to the tune of billions in borrowed money.

American Perversity
Sex, Politics and Religion

$ Set the record for most executions by any governor in American history.

$ Became president after losing the popular vote by more than 500,000 votes...

Accomplishments as president:

$ Attacked and took over two countries.

$ Spent the surplus and bankrupted the treasury.

$ Shattered the record for biggest annual deficit in history. Set economic record for most private bankruptcies filed in any 12-month period. Set all-time record for biggest drop in the history of the stock market.

We'll be right back.

"This just in, Tom... I'm over at Art's Deli in Studio City—where I just finished my favorite, the bagel and lox plate—across from the Bank of America, which was held up last week and I realize now that I inadvertently asked the Emmy-winning star of the police drama *The Shield*, Michael Chicklis to watch my things while I went inside to wash my hands. He and a lady friend, a dog at their feet, said sure.

"Now Tom, this wasn't in the script (nor was my conversation with Tom, in case you were wondering), but I wondered something as I went inside to use the restroom. I wondered what the man who carries the shield on TV would have done at the scene of that crime. What a scene that might have made: "art meets life over a deli sandwich." Live from Studio City, reporting from Art's Delicatessen, I'm Bradford Borden. Back to you, Tom..."

Finally, in the "Records and References" section of 'W's' resume, we have the following:

• At least one conviction for drunken driving in Maine (Texas driving record has been erased and is not available).

• AWOL from the National Guard.

• All records of tenure as governor of Texas have been spirited away to father's library, sealed in secrecy and are unavailable for public view.

William Bradford Borden

- All records of any SEC investigations into insider trading or bankrupt companies are sealed in secrecy and unavailable for public view.

"That's all for the president's resume. We'll see you at the polls...

Wait ...before we go, the last thing before we head into the seventh chapter, and this writing dialogue is not my forte, and I apologize for the pseudo-parody. I am tired of this writing-pen. It's a lightweight and I am tired of lightweights and maybe that is why I'm frazzled and scattered, overloaded and overwhelmed, just dealing with all the minutiae, the trivial pursuits, the lightweights. Yes, that is much of the stress, or causes thereof—all the psychosomatic headaches in the trivial and banal search for meaning, and meaning to achieve greatness but not sure of all the categories—so, invariably many chose the lightweight division.

Do you remember a time when the Golden Rule was, "Do unto others as you would have them do unto you?" Do you remember those days? But now the rule has changed and, like most sequels, the new one isn't nearly as good, or golden.

The new Golden Rule doesn't come from the greatest, the original, the old. No, the new rules were made by a bunch of babies. Their booming voices shouted in their fear of a fair game, "He who has the gold rules..." But their voices shriveled. They had created a rule that was meant to be broken.

What is it that divides us so, not only amongst others, but also amongst ourselves? And "others" and "ourselves" could be inter-changed. But can we change? Do we seek change? Have you got change? And $48.25, the change from a $50, sits on the green outside table, under a receipt, under a coffee cup, and many people pass by and I like it being there.

Brother can you spare a dime? No, but I'll give you a 10. Ten, yes, 10, a minion of hope—opening the timeless, digging much deeper, wishing all well, and there were many maps, many signs, and many decisions. Cutting off the arm to save the self and then repelling. Is that repelling to you? Do you want me to back off?

American Perversity
Sex, Politics and Religion

And there are many decisions, and the cutting off, like a human smorgasbord of leftovers from a "bris," Sephardim and Ashkenazi. And the choices, presented by the moil (he was also the head chef), his butcher knife in hand. And you had to hand it to the moil, he had a sharp wit—razor-sharp—and with a glint in his eyes he said, "Decide."

What were the choices again? Decide! We've got homicide, fratricide and suicide. Not much of a selection, I'd say! Isn't there a special? Why not try something else? This restaurant is run by a coalition of lightweights. Let's go to Club Hedonism and try a piece of that peace.

I have a memory like an elephant, and I remember once, going to a donkey barbecue where everyone got a piece of ass. People were doing unto others and there were no rules. There was ass for breakfast, lunch and dinner—even dessert.

Bush, no, I can't write about that right after that—bush after dessert, and "beating around the bush" is what we so often do, instead of discussing what really matters at the main course. And often, after dessert, there is just social intercourse and that is acceptable; there is kinship. But, so often, it is ephemeral, the community and communication guarded, and there is barbed wire. A wire so thin, but still it is there, restraining and containing us and we are often afraid to change and move up a division. So we run and hide and lose ourselves, lost in space as we long for depth, we long for sustenance, and we long for meaning. Waiter, can I have another menu?

94

7
Go For Broke

"The Greatest Generation," what an awesomely profound concept. Good, better, best, and like Rather, Jennings and Brokaw we rate things—comparatives and superlatives, trying to quantify quality. There is a quality to quantity that we measure and judge, and the model parade continues and I'll put my Studio City up against your South Beach any time.

The time is 7:23 (19:23), and a stunning Angelina Jolie-type promenades north. She is now East to my West and she is sitting with some rocker-type and I know she can rock and she loves to roll—maybe on hay in a late summer, but more on feathers, taking flight on the bed as she lies down to watch the TV news "The Iraq Watch."

She likes the sound of that on Brokaw's lips, and she looks into the full length, gold-trimmed closet mirror that faces her bed, but now it's mine—she's on my bed, a full queen, and there is no TV. It was she who lustfully—for she is a lover of lust, a lustful lover—said, "That's right, I rock. Do you wanna watch?"

I wonder what instrument she plays as I tug at the heavy chain that hangs around her olive neck and the silver cross that both connects and divides her breasts. They are full and she licks her lips and dims the light. Only the bathroom door is ajar and Egyptian musk incense burns and so does her fire within and without.

She's ready to play, another song, song and dance, a possible triple threat ready for a triple play, waiting to perform. She is in top form—the yoga and aerobics are helpful—but it is more than

William Bradford Borden

intercourse, the main course. She will be social later, but now she is a slut, a Madonna and a whore, and she says, "bye bye" and it is opposite—the way we've become. She likes to fuck and run, run and fuck, and so this time we just fucked with our minds.

I hope you don't mind, but it is part of the allure, the catching and letting go, giving and taking, fucking and forgetting. And do we ever, is it possible, or are they always in your sexual psyche—the people we've fucked? And the word "fucked" is becoming more universal, as perhaps we've come to the point where nobody gives a fuck. And I question and I ask, is it better to give or to receive? Who gives a fuck? I sure as hell do, and I never forget.

How is a generation defined? Is it 10 or 20 years? Who's keeping score? When Lincoln spoke at Gettysburg (during the time of another great generation) he established a date and time. Subtraction was necessary to look back to the past and we can add to the equation. 2003 minus 1865 (four score and seven years ago) and we knew it was subtraction because of the word "ago," a go. A go-go? Who gave it the go? Do the math, and a "score" then was 20 years, four score and seven would be 87.

Because I've roughly established 1865 for Lincoln's address, we can subtract 87 from 1865 and get the reference point, the "ago," or moment in history that Lincoln referred points one to 1778. So maybe the speech at Gettysburg was delivered in 1863, which would put the "four score and seven years ago" at 1776, and displays of fireworks would become the tradition of America: a tradition of independence, power and responsibility.

What is your response to responsibility? Do you have the ability to respond? It has been said and written and even realized that with freedom comes responsibility; and so, you might ask, "Is everyone meant to be free?" What is it that binds us and constrains us? What is it that restrains us and hinders our balance of freedom and responsibility?

These are just rhetorical questions. I am not expecting to give or receive a response, but I want to be responsible in my endeavors. I want to have freedom to speak and to observe. I want to honor my father and mother, to honor the greatest generation. I want to move up to their division and close the divide. I want to think four score

American Perversity
Sex, Politics and Religion

and seven in the past and four score and seven in the future, and I will stop for math, because I enjoy numbers and their challenge and direction—the equations; one subtraction, one addition, one past, one future, with a base in the present. And the present is now. It is always now. When? You got it. Where? You'll find it. Who? You'll know. What? It's your choice. Why? You'll decide.

I am on the tail end of the baby boomers, one of the last, a 1961 model, a product of the greatest, and I've been raised on new math. My 3rd grade math teacher was a buxom Greek goddess who instilled in me the importance of multiplication; I learned to love to multiply. How philosophical in retrospect—from a product of Greece, my appreciation of the times came.

I've always thought it significant that the multiplication of two negatives created positives. How is your energy? Have you checked your numbers and figures? Does it all compute or is the computer doing all the brain training for you and in the process draining your brain. Yeah, you can flush your troubles down the drain, but all the chemicals affect the well and the effect is profound. I think I even actually effectively distinguished between the effects and affects.

Who does your books? Do you do your own? Do you do unto others? What are your rules? And I continue to ask questions of you and myself, looking for answers while taking pleasure in the quest, the lust and the passion for figuring it all out. And "all" would suggest wholeness, completion and integrity. That is the response. The answer and the outcome that most of us desire—a true continuum of events—positives, negatives and neutrals; future, past and present; and it is probable, given a margin of error of plus or minus three percent.

And we begin to gallop along, here in the moment, riding into the sunset, and was it sunny where you were today? And who and what were you today? Where are you and more importantly why are you? Try to figure these things out and, in the process, pray for a productive outcome as you try to solve the riddle of the most profound equation of existence...

"Four score and seven years ago..." Do the math. For me my date will always be different than yours and that concept—of arriving in this world at a given place and then departing at another—is utterly

William Bradford Borden

equal to space and time, as well as computer and computee, and external and internal. So, what is your equation? New and old math... Mine is this 2003 minus 87 and 2003 plus 87, just looking for perspective.

The future equation is obvious and easy and the answer is 2090, when I will be 129 years old; can you imagine? Yes, I wrote, "I will," and with medicine and change that is possible, but unlikely—would you like that? Eternity? A beginning, middle, but no end...

So, if there is no end then where is the middle? Is it east or west? With no ends, finding a location becomes difficult and challenges us perhaps to question eternity. But, instead, we look at our work and our works, our passions and our creations, our self and our souls, and calculate our relevance, our substance, and our significance.

It is all of our destinies—not just Americans—but a world of mathematicians trying to figure it all out. Human rubrics in a cerebral sea of souls held in balance by the timeless trick of synapses fueled by blood, and it is a good thing—these problems and their solvers, some of them morons, some savants, and amazingly—many are oxymoron's. Bloody good people...

The pen is different today, thicker and seemingly more powerful than the previous model. This weapon is a Pentel R.S.V.P. BK 90 USA Fine pen. How do you find products made in the USA? Have we been digging so deep for gold in America that we have finally hit China, and instead of the bars being stamped with USA, we use a stamp of China? The transition is complete. The transition is from a geo-political world to geo-economic one, the transition from the Far East to the Middle, from Vietnam to a couple of rounds in the Gulf. Dollars and sense, a penny saved is a penny earned, and another for your thoughts...

I won't even go further with this because I'm not an economist and, in fact, although I do have a fairly competent business mind, I am no businessman—no show business, monkey business, or funny business—just my business. Mind?

Back to you, Tom, and the drum beats of war, the tom-toms beat—and that ranks with the worst of transitions and no one said that transitions would be easy—our focus so often blurred by interruptions and commercials. What are you buying? What are the products?

American Perversity
Sex, Politics and Religion

Where are they made? Do you question creation and all the inventions and innovations, trying to figure it all out?

I was going to share what Hollywood.com said about Brokaw, but the paper has blown away. First north toward Mexicali, then east toward Universal Studios; and one could question whether there is truth at Universal, universal truth.

Isn't it strange, it seems to me, when people say "well"—well, well, well—"well to tell you..." Maybe they want to wax poetic in their contradiction, "well to tell you the truth..." Oh please do tell; tell well.

To tell you the truth, when people tell me that they're telling me the truth, I question the consequences of my belief in their story and I question, and then I stop to question myself and ask, "Who am I to question?"

Do you question the media, the message and the messenger? Has your village gone global and do you trot? Are you hot? How's the weather? Whether we want to believe that weather is important—is it relevant to ask? How is your relative humidity? Are you moist? Are you affluent? Is your cup running over?

Yes, how is your business, if you don't mind, and how is your health? Have you been given a clean one and, may I ask, who's paying the bill?

Shabbat Shalom. It is Saturday the 10th, the day of rest, and today many people will rest more, get up later, and many—the intelligentsia for sure—will read the newspapers in search of messages and meanings. In the rack to my left sits the newspaper that I grew up with and so loved as a child, *The New York Times*, and right at that moment a Latino man comes in with the Sunday Preview of the *Los Angeles Times*.

I wonder if Los Angeles times are different than New York ones. They are both American, both coastal and both markedly more liberal than the majority of the country.

The root of the word "liberal" has its roots in freedom, for "liberare" is the Latin for "free." And it is an interesting juxtaposition—liberal and conservative, left with the right. And is it right what we are left with, in our pursuit of pie, of America and ourselves, and in the process of conservation impede the conversation

William Bradford Borden

with the soul, and in the process take away our liberty and our need to be liberal?

Yes, what are you trying to conserve? A statue of antiquity, maybe, but is your statue, your object, your art—is this statue liberated, made in France, maybe, by people who know the power of balance?

A balance most obvious in the tug of the sexes; and I again am reminded of telling my dear friend, the Catherine Zeta-Jones look-alike, that my former Italian girlfriend was a real nymph. And I say that with fondness, with a smile and I remember the advice given in Italy for marrying an Italian woman: getting in the bargain a whore in the bedroom, a chef in the kitchen and a maid in the house. But, hey, do we ever really get what we bargain for? And to "Catherine" I said that "Roma" was not half as pretty, but twice as sexy.

How sexy are you? Are you conserving or liberating? West Side or East? Uptown or down? Right or wrong? Left or right? And is there right in wrong, and if we're right about what is wrong does that make it right? What do you hold up? What do you raise in praise?

Wouldn't that make a terrific headline to see that a sexy French broad—statuesque and liberal, a bit green with envy, but not of penises—had seen her share, and she had hardened. That had never been her problem; she could keep it up with the best of them and she was a special gift—a gift of love from masters of love, professors of the profound.

She was conceived, perhaps, on the West Bank, looking out at Paris, the Seine, with a little extra baguette and a glass of red wine. And like a good woman, liberal at times and conservative at others, she came to make a stand, torch in hand, right arm raised, love power, and a piece of that was for all, and she sent a message and the message of the gift was profound. The message of the gift, to N.Y., to America, to the world, the message was, "Give me your ..."

What will be printed on your marker, your stone, your statue? "All the news that's fit to print" is printed in the left box corner of the top of the *New York Times*.

I remember in journalism class being told about the editors who wrote headlines and how important they were. That is easy to understand because these headlines become like the title of a book or

American Perversity
Sex, Politics and Religion

the marquee of a movie theater, but these campaigns are just for the day... "Fit to print," for a moment of time, a day in the life, and what are your headlines today?

Look around you; look, if you will, look to the wells. What are the messages and who are the messengers? Are they liberating or conserving? Are they giving or taking? And I thought of the term "Indian giver" and the implications there. What about other ethnic slurs—to "Jew someone down," to "get gypped." And people say these things, words perhaps, but with deeper meaning they don't even understand. So what do your headlines proclaim; have you read the paper today? Do you like to read? Do you even know what you like and what you don't like? Like it or not, it matters. And are your matters personal or private, liberal or conservative, human or divine?

What does it say in the paper on the days after you can no longer read when the circulation has stopped; yes, what does it say when your address has changed permanently and they're writing about you? Who are they, they that write about those who have moved and passed on? What beauty with words the *New York Times* writers gave in tribute to the 911 victims.

Do you have a victim mentality? What is your state? Do you belong to a union? Have you been to a good funeral lately? How about a bris or a baptism? Have you been to quincenera or perhaps a sweet sixteen in the pursuit of one-upmanship? How about a wake or a memorial? Beginning, middle and end—trying to measure up to great expectations, but often settling for mediocre or good...

Do you have a good coffee-table book or maybe a great one; and, in greatness, do you play with words or, instead, the remote control and someone else's? What else do you do? Find a great book. I think they have a book of the compilation of the obituaries that the *Times* ran for the thousands that blew away, cremated against their will, and breathed in by their brethren, New Yorkers, Americans, humans.

I am reminded of a friend, an Army Reserve colonel and a civilian prison dentist. A true leader, soldier and American, he used to say, "The Devil is in the details," and I wonder now if he ever told a rapist, a murderer or a thief—when they were on Novocain instead of cocaine and the steel instruments were in their mouths, and they had

101

William Bradford Borden

to be silent, but you could still smell their seething shit—I wonder if he ever told these inmates they were getting superior medical and dental treatment than probably 90% of their fellow Americans.

I wonder if the colonel when he worked on the captives, ever admonished that the "Devil was in the details." Maybe the devil was, actually—quite probably when you look at the priorities—"more" in the details, because perhaps the devil was more there—in the human steel lockbox—and not, unfortunately, in the human social lockbox. Have you locked yourself out lately? Have you been locked out, locked up, and locked down?

What about people we lock up? Lots of blacks for drug offenses, trying to supply the natural, homegrown holistic products, but no competition for the prescription drug cartels—beaten by big business, white power and almighty God. And on the back of our bills, our dollars, our greenbacks, there is a proclamation "In God We Trust." Who is your God? Do you trust God with your finances so you can give a 10 percent tip? Is God picking up the mortgage, the car payment, or your student loan?

How is it, then, that the corporate scandals of the telecommunication and energy and even accounting companies—big businesses in general—is often far more destructive in theory than the inner city black businesses, trying to make a buck, trusting in God? And I am certainly not advocating another Amsterdam just justice. Is justice just? Just think about it, the way we lock people away, hunting down the hunters, raging testosterone, and we lock them away. Unless, of course, they can play and then we let them slay. How about a glass of O.J.?

If our dollars proclaim "In God We Trust," who then is paying the defense of the predator-priest-pedophiles who prefer the confession box to the lock, think outside the box. The priests lips are locked but others are not, and knotted up are the souls of the parishioners as the collection plate is passed over and across and the priests says "In God We Trust" and everyone says "Amen!" And that last "Amen" gives him an idea as he follows the alter boy to take off his robes.

This chapter is probably the most tangential and off-course that I have written thus far. "Where is Brokaw?" you might question. I guess what I am attempting is fair and honest journalism, just making

American Perversity
Sex, Politics and Religion

some observations. Back to the middle, east of here, to N. Y, the middle for me between Los Angeles and London. There is so much power in all three, Los Angeles, New York and London—cities with a common connection of English.

Yes, back to N.Y. and today's headlines—some having happened yesterday, others in the infinite past, some initiated in the snap of a finger, and others in the agenda of a lifetime. And New York, holding Los Angeles and London in balance, the scales of the Western world, pounds and stones, inches and feet, fish and chips—we'll do it our way, thank you very much.

If you make it where? Yes, where? Do you know exactly where you are? What are you wearing and what is more important to you, what you are wearing or where you are wearing it? And it all comes down to the reporter's questions: Who, What, Where, When and Why, trying to put together the story, to tell it like it is.

A homeless man, whom I have talked to before, all the way from New York, and he looks like he could be Pacino's brother, a homeless brother, and I greet him and want to let him know he matters as he sits on the comfortable chair to drink his coffee, and I collect my books to move outside to enjoy the sun going down. Now he is inside and I am out, and I wonder if we all really do have choices when we're told that we do.

When I give him the dollar—and a silent blessing—this octogenarian with oversized glasses that cover half of her sagging, cartoon-like face, and with duck-like lips, spatters something about how, "We in Studio City... (Who the fuck is "we" I want to ask) support the homeless in other ways by finding them work and places to live."

She is self-righteous in her tone, and I think to myself that these people "we" support don't want to work, they don't want a place, they are hunters and gatherers, gathering and hunting. I wonder if the price of aluminum increases with inflation, and I'm happy, so happy, as I look behind me into the Starbucks. The Al Pacino stand-in is sitting, and I feel even better that I responded to the sanctimonious bitch.

"He's from N.Y. and he's a human being, and maybe if you talked to him you would know," I tell her as piercingly as possible, but she

103

William Bradford Borden

doesn't know the power of fools but I do. I tell her he is part of the fabric of our society and he makes a difference. I hope you feel good woman (and I won't call you "lady") as you pass out your cans and your soup along with your judgment. Why don't you try a little laughter, a little hope, and a little love?

Pacino's stand-in, I realize, is most probably a Vietnam Veteran. I know the type first hand, a war that has kept a generation on patrol, ambushing and retreating into the jungle of life, and I wonder what kind of role the Gulf War veterans will play. Will it be well scripted or symptomatic of the times? The sagging, self-righteous cartoon leaves now, and "Pacino's" also gone, both out patrolling, heading towards different sectors one going west the other going east—trying to meet up with their respective parties.

Back in New York, Tom Brokaw marked his 20-year anniversary as the anchor of NBC News on Sept. 5, 2003. And so September comes with mixed blessings—the good with the not so good—like returning to school after summer vacation. September, a time for atoning and celebrating, mourning and remembering—cards for everything, and now another. Did someone call 9-1-1? And there had been signs but no cards. Happy Anniversary, Happy New Year and Mazel Tov!

In an earlier chapter, I mentioned the NBC journalist David Bloom, who died in Iraq and who lived next door to the son of my mother's friend. Bloom left behind a wife, Melanie, and two daughters. Father's Day would never be the same for the girls. Of course there were cards for such occasions, but Tom Brokaw in his eulogy and tribute to David Bloom wrote and spoke his own words, and they were more powerful than any speeding bullet or swashbuckling sword, for certainly Brokaw had long known the power of words and the person and that, in so many ways, the pen really is; yes, the pen is…

Back to you, Tom, and the David Bloom eulogy and the sound, I would imagine, was resonant and godly. But what is that to be like God and deliver a message, a messenger of good and evil? And even if the messenger was humble and kind, there was still power in the pulpit, and the journalist's weapon was his mind and his pen, his voice and his eyes, his wisdom and foolishness.

American Perversity
Sex, Politics and Religion

It is a difficult segues to Brokaw's message because it is so utterly profound. The sounds his carefully chosen words must have made by this anointed messenger in God's house, in a cathedral named after the Irish saint, Patrick. And God bless the Irish, master storytellers and masters of survival. And in God's house, the prophet spoke. It was an April day in New York City and the subject of the in-depth report was a fellow reporter, a David, a Bloom, and I'm sure Brokaw must have been a mentor to Bloom, and he spoke with such affection about a journalist covering Gulf II, up close and personal. And it was not the bullets that plucked up this man, this bloom, cut off so young; no, not bullets but blood, which perhaps because of restriction, constriction, and pressure, no longer circulated. The well of life was shut off, and I wondered what had happened to all the affluence.

In that vein, this is what the prophet, Tom, said of the rising star, David, the fallen bloom, the fallen messenger. "I have long believed—and I have said this before in war colleges and other military settings—that warriors and journalists share the same gene pool. Now, some warriors don't always like to hear that. They know, for example, that we have better expense accounts. But we all like unconventional lives. Journalists and warriors thrive on catching the bad guys."

Powerful words delivered by the master messenger, master of ceremony, the Master Brokaw. I just thought of a wonderful idea, Brokaw for President. With strong support from New York and California and, with the Midwest the balance, I'm sure he could win. And like Reagan, having been well-rehearsed, he was ready for his close-up and so were we, wanting not so much fools wisdom, mixed messages and distortion, but instead a prophet, a messenger and a leader to tell it like it is; and, how it could be.

I'm sorry for my political tangent, but we all—according to the character in Malamud's brilliant book *The Fixer*—in the end, to end our imprisonment, must be political people. It's just too bad politics has become so political, and it's even sadder that the quality of life, in search for equality, we're told, is quantified in such a problematic way that the divide grows greater as deficits blossom, and the dream dims.

105

William Bradford Borden

But there is hope in Los Angeles and in New York and in America that the two coasts will get together and do the most to share with everyone in between a dream of America. American Dreams: day and night dreams, black and white dreams, north and south, east and west, Compton and Harlem, Rodeo Drive and Park Avenue, East Los Angeles and East Harlem, Ellis Island and L.A. American Dreams.

Made all over the world and transplanted to the magical land, the happiest place on earth, a big Red Apple. And an apple a day, even in L.A., just might be the thing that rings true to the dreams, seeds and trees, reaping and sewing, blooming and flowering.

…Brokaw continued his tribute to Bloom…

"We can live off the land, when necessary. We have a chain of command, but we're not shy about challenging it. And battles are won and great stories are uncovered from the ground up, down in the dirt, not in the air-conditioned comfort of the studios. Moreover, warriors and journalists are irreplaceable components in the structure of a constitutional republic ensuring national security and the right of the people to know what their government is doing in their name and their interests."

What amazing writing. If Brokaw were chosen we might finally have a messenger, a prophet, and a president who just might write his own material.

Who writes your material? Who's your director? What roles have you chosen? What role has chosen you? Do your Sundays flow into your Mondays or is the transition from weekend to weekday, from work to play and back again difficult? What difficulties are you having? Is life that difficult and is it made this way so we can create our own conflicts and resolutions?

So many questions, and yet as reporters and warriors both know, our days are numbered and there is only a finite number of conflicts a normal mortal can fight. I guess that the issue becomes in your definition of self.

What do you prefer in your pursuit of enlightenment? Do you prefer the logical or the spiritual, the mortal or the divine, the what? I can't think, or actually, I think of many but they are my juxtapositions, not yours. What gives you balance and tugs at your heart and soul?

American Perversity
Sex, Politics and Religion

Do you prefer making love and the transcendent, reincarnate death of orgasm, or do you prefer to make war in pursuit of the hunt, trying to find your own balance of good and evil while lusting for power? What lasts longer the love or the power? Is it the 11th hour where you are; is it pushing midnight or noon, sunrise or sunset, beginning, middle or end?

So many questions in this chapter—aren't there? That is one of the beauties of writing, reporting live, from the moment—space and time. In your current space and time do you feel connected to your fellow man, to your brothers and sisters, to your families and friends, nuclear and extended? If connected, how close and current? If separated, how far and by how many degrees?

If I wanted to get this chapter to Brokaw, how separated by degrees am I from this conceivable concept? To my mother one, to her friend two, to Melanie Bloom three, to Brokaw four. Four degrees in a mathematical example of connections, some more separate, others less equal, some in degrees and others in moments, and the magic of the moment was not that anything was possible, but instead that there was a divinity within, wanting to create, wanting to connect; wanting to be wanted.

What would you want if you had virtually everything you needed and you made the $7 million a year that Brokaw reportedly makes and were responsible and prudent like I'm sure he is? He certainly seems like a man who reads lots of books, and has even written several to include the terrific *The Greatest Generation,* from which I carry that concept. Yes, Tom Brokaw truly appears to be a man of real virtues.

How is your quality of life? Could it be better? I'm sure, like most of us, it could be worse, and much of this concept just becomes semantics, with comparatives and superlatives being the measure of our messages—good, better, best…Matters of perspective and what mattered more than just about anything was the perspective and the point of view because the degrees of separation were often infinite, but also finite, and we couldn't see how far, yet how very close we really were.

I'm reminded of some experiment in the Pacific with some monkeys who did something on an island and others, miles away in a greatly compacted time frame, followed suit. A true example of space

William Bradford Borden

and time with no physical and perceived contact; but there was a connection and impact, nevertheless, and the communication was evoked with a sense of transcendence and mysticism, and so right now I have had a form of that experience—a communicative epiphany, if you will.

Do you feel caught in the middle? Sometimes like me, like a middle child wanting to do better? We move, or don't we? And we transition from good to better to best, from local reporter to national, from morning to night.

There is heaviness in the air in this Age of Aquarius and the hope for goodness and levity seems rapidly disappearing. That is disappointing but it certainly gives us time to reevaluate all our dreams and ambitions. Where am I going with this chapter and this book? Not only am I questioning you, the reader, but also just as profoundly I am questioning myself.

It is hard to write when I am down, but it is the lows that brings me the highs, the pain that brings the depth. It is the expression and the communication of these ideas that help me to heal myself. It is this expression that gives me a greater understanding of the world and myself.

On page eight of nine pages of a downloaded *Midwest Today* by Larry Jordan, I just flipped the page and at the top of the page was a question to Brokaw, and the question was "What makes you happy?" Do you ever really ask yourself that question? Yeah, what really makes you happy? What makes you feel good about who you are and what you do? What can you do, what can I do, what can we do, to live happier more fulfilled lives? Ask yourself what makes you happy?

Brokaw's response, reporting from his heart, "Oh a variety of things makes me happy, beginning with my family. I happen to have had, I think, one of the great marriages in the history of that institution." Wow! As much as I rail against the institution of marriage, how utterly divine and beautiful it can be when it really works.

I wonder why, with so many people around, I feel like such an island, even though, I've been told, that no man is one. Why then do I feel deserted, feeling so close to paradise yet far from reality? And

American Perversity
Sex, Politics and Religion

maybe others feel the same way and that is the reason the evening news seems overwhelmingly supported by prescription drug pushers; and I wonder what went wrong, but perhaps more importantly, I wonder what we can do to right the wrongs.

Brokaw, in my opinion could right those wrongs in the office of president. Just imagine, "President Brokaw." I wonder if he would even consider it. Have you, like so many others, given up on politics and politicians with the realization that big business and special interests are what dictate our lives and not, unfortunately, a better quality of life? Whose business is that? All of ours I'd say.

Right now there is Corona and tequila induced shouting and laughter across the street at Mexicali—and I wonder why young people in America have to, it seems, rely on excessive alcohol consumption to express their inner demons and desires—searching for happiness, laughter and escape but so often missing the magic of the moment.

I would imagine that the moments of a happy marriage go by quickly and the anniversaries come more rapidly, as the moments become memories, headstones replace milestones, and obituaries replace scripts.

Brokaw continues, in the story of his life, to the question "What makes you happy?" and it is interesting to me that his answer is humble and there is no covert ego. He seems like a truly grateful, fortunate and happy man. He continues, 'I have an extraordinarily accomplished wife; we met when we were 15 years of age, we have grown together, I have learned so much from her..."

Yes, I would imagine that there is real truth behind great women behind great men and the mutual support that is possible, and yet I question mutual dependence and the ramifications of co-dependency. I have been so touched by the effect of divorce on so many of my students. They express the loss and the hurt, in their poetry and prose, and so many times they have cried and brought tears to listeners in their reflections and revelations of what divorce has done to them.

Assuredly, the family is an important institution, and yet its very existence in California, in America, and in the world for that matter (and I would suggest it matters much more than we realize) is greatly troubled and in jeopardy. Commitment is certainly a major variable.

William Bradford Borden

As I have written before, there is something (if not a great deal) to be said for structure and routine. These factors, structure and routine, are often the basis of commitment, marriage and family. Maslow's "Hierarchy of Needs," proposes that it is difficult, if not virtually impossible, to progress to the next level of wants and desires in the pursuit of self-actualizing, if our physical needs are not first met. This, in fact, is where family plays such an integral role.

I'm not advocating that we go around with sardonic smiles on our faces when we are sad, because sadness is a part of life and without sadness happiness is less appreciated. Conflict and resolution, highs and lows, ups and downs, are certainly all important; but the self-actualizing, nirvana state, a kind of heaven on earth, certainly seems desirable to me.

What are your dreams and desires? Is your life a living hell and the lows, the downs, not the down lows, or the low downs, but the nadirs and bottoms, is that where you are? Be your own reporter. Investigate. Try to solve and resolve the conflicts and move on, to higher ground. Ask yourself those questions—the who's, the what's, the where's, the why's and the when's; and when you have done this I think you will realize that you're reporting about the most important subject, in the most profound drama, in the most amazing class of your life, and your job is that of student, teacher and master.

Do you like your work, or do you have to work on liking it and in the process become slave to a syllabus of deception and regret, selling yourself like a cheap whore and in essence getting fucked without enjoyment? Yes, what do you do? Brokaw talks of his work and relates, "What makes me happy is a job well done here on a daily basis." How significant and awesome that—like a great athlete, a superstar, an icon—is the day-to-day commitment to excellence, to work and to the game of life people like Tom Brokaw make.

Today is Wednesday, and in a week of seven, with Sunday being the first day, Wednesday falls directly in the middle, as it does in the typical workweek of Monday through Friday where Wednesday is right in the middle—the climax perhaps in the drama model of life. Day-by-day, a week-by-week, a group of seven, and Wednesday is in the middle. It is an arbitrary measure, but a measurement nonetheless.

American Perversity
Sex, Politics and Religion

Do you measure up? Do you plot your progression or progress without a plot, falling prey but without a prayer to who you are and what you should be? And as you drive in to a job that's driving you crazy you try to find a song to sing along to. But instead you are subjected to the idle chatter of idle chatterers who remind you that it is Wednesday, it is "hump day," and that you are over the hump. I wonder will you hump tonight.

Will this be the climax of your week as you shuffle into work—like Quasimodo waiting for the bell to ring—and work so hard to produce a product that you don't even believe in so you can make other people rich, who don't really care about you, as they cut your benefits, increase your responsibility, decrease your salary, and raise theirs?

Do you do all this so you can get to the weekend—to let it all go, so you can start again? A routine of madness, but then you're saving for retirement, so you can go to Paris, and Notre Dame, and by then you might be too old to climb up the cathedral and look at the gargoyles. And will you remember when you were at university and you read Hugo and felt empathy for Quasimodo, the consummate underdog?

And as you walk toward the Latin quarter in the City of Love and realize it is Wednesday, will you go back to your hotel and make love or will you look into the mirror and ask yourself who you are, where you are going tomorrow, when you'll be happy, and why you didn't ask these questions earlier, as the drama moves into a fade-out over the Seine, looking toward the Eiffel Tower and the ultimate denouement?

I am humbled by my words because I feel as though I am judging you and I apologize for that. I am recently saddened, down and unclear about the direction of America and our place in the world. I realize this chapter is off course of the subject, and yet, I feel inspired by Brokaw, to report and in essence send my own message here.

Do you question your character? Will you question mine? Do you find my erotica and my attitude offensive? Are you an offensive or defensive person? Questions, questions, questions and yes, I could give you answers, answers, answers, but what about commentary, analysis and synthesis? What really lies beneath all the tit for tat and

111

William Bradford Borden

more importantly, are we lying to one another and ourselves when our response to the questions is that it doesn't really matter?

What is the matter with you, with me, with us? What is the difference between a monster and a matter baby? "What's a 'matter baby'?" you might wonder. "Nothing's the matter baby."

Thank you for allowing me that comic aside, and I hope you have a comic side. I remember reading that "laughter is the best medicine" and so I hope that you will laugh today and find the levity and irony of life and be in the moment—that fine line between laughter and tears. Laughing so hard you cry, yet knowing there are times when the reverse may be true, crying into laughter, striking a balance without striking out, but instead playing your hardest with heart and soul.

How is your heart and soul? The more I write and reflect and look at the life of Brokaw I understand the power of soul mates. I saw it in my mother and father, as well, and it gives me hope. And even though I still tend to think in terms of soul mates, in the plural, I think I am making progress, and I begin to appreciate now and see the concept of mutual support, which for me comes in the soul mate sense of woman, and it is now becoming just as much a need as a want in my search for balance and search for self.

In *Midwest Today*, Larry Jordan recounts, "Tom had been dating a pretty girl whom he later married, named Meredith Auld, who won the title of Miss South Dakota. Tom interviewed her on the air, and after he finished, he was so excited he accidentally left his microphone on. When he told her he loved her, it went out over the air for all to hear!"

Isn't that what all of us need in this Age of Aquarius, to hear that we are loved and to know that someone cares? To prefer giving rather than receiving and, in the process, receive the ultimate gift of being in the present and living for the moment? Not necessarily to negate hate and evil in the world and their importance in tugging at our hearts and pulling at our souls as we strive to be better people, better Americans and better human beings. And in that being, that sense of mortality has the profound possibility of transcending to future generations, to future greatness, to future immortality.

American Perversity
Sex, Politics and Religion

It is an awesome responsibility that we must embrace and endure in our search for the good, the better and the best, as we learn our lessons from the past, experience them in the present, and plan for the future. Like good reporters we must question our directions—individual and collective—as we play our roles in the most important broadcast of our lives; and it is live—there are no commercial interruptions. Back to you Tom.

SEXSHUN III: RELIGION

116

8

Far From Mary

Today is the 15th of May 2003, and the moon is in Scorpio. The moon is full and there will also be a lunar eclipse. And I feel somehow that this affects my moods and my feelings as I shift into the eighth of ten chapters, the fourth of an estimated five journals, and the fourth, of I'm not sure of how many significant pens. And the pens are my instruments and with them I attempt to play with words and express...

I'm stuck on what I'm attempting to express... Do you ever feel that way, where you've got so much to relate and to share but you're not sure how or why?

Why not? Why not what? God, I am trying, and in Italian there is an expression that is often used when one is frustrated, and that expression, from the Italians—the masters of the non-verbal, but a spoken language of unparalleled rhythm and beauty—is "Madonna mia"—my Madonna.

This chapter is dedicated to Madonna—not the one of the Italian expression, which comes from the Catholic Church, which comes from Rome, but instead this is another Madonna—an American Madonna and an international icon.

This chapter already seems so stilted and contrived, and I hope most of this book doesn't feel that way; but as I often tell my students—think on the paper; get right into it. And writer's write, and usually we will begin class with a journal on a topic or subject (and they are basically the same) that I've written on the board.

117

William Bradford Borden

From the very beginning of my classes I talk about language and the components that are integral to almost every language—components that are reciprocal in nature: reading and writing; speaking and listening. And, yet, there is a fifth element that is of equal or rather cumulative import, and that element is thinking. Have you ever thought of that? Think about it. Think about what? Exactly.

My beloved students: future pharmacists, veterinarians, doctors, lawyers, teachers, actors, strippers, fathers, mothers, alcoholics, drug addicts, murderers, prophets, soldiers, dentists, businessmen, scholars...who presently are all those things and so much more.

I have to blame my mood on the moon and the lunatic in my almost 75 percent body of water, which almost exactly matches the amount of water on the earth, and all the water inside of me, like the tides in Malibu, Salt Lake and South Beach. Hell, I don't even know if the Salt Lake has tides, but my tides are high and low, and that was the essence of the journal prompt, which was:

"Write about what makes you happy and what makes you sad. Are you basically an optimist or a pessimist, and have you ever been very depressed? If so, how do you deal with that?"

Needless to say, it did not set the tone for the most uplifting of classes, as I would imagine it is not doing much to set the tone for the most uplifting of chapters; but, as I've stated before, these lows are almost certainly essential to appreciate the highs, and I would assert that they are even more magnificent when they are completely free of any mind-or mood-altering substances—synthetic or natural.

This whole thing is getting me down, but by writing and thinking about it I am able to come to some observations and revelations that are at least pertinent to me. I feel so unsure of so much these days; and again, I blame it partly on the moon, for tonight it is full, and in Scorpio, and eclipsing. It is like me, for I am full—a perpetual optimist, whose cup runs over and then is left half empty as pessimism sets in and I search for new sustenance. Do you know who you are? Or, do you take cover in the one-dimensional paradigm of self? Maybe, that is the most selfish thing we can ever do—not explore all of our dimensions and possibilities. Is that possible? If

118

American Perversity
Sex, Politics and Religion

there were a third dimension, wouldn't the fourth be a total, all around perspective of balance and wisdom.

In essence, when you think about it, our lives are one huge advertising campaign with the product *us*. And around us the slogans, the mantras, the wording: "Just Do It;" "If It's Borden, It's Got to Be Good;" the "All the News That's Fit to Print." And all of the letters, words and ideas, create an image, perceived and real, internal and external, priceless and worthless.

Yes, these campaigns help create interest in our products and help us create worth and value, but it often seems that the problem in the marketing is that in devising our advertising campaigns we are not completely aware of our own. So, what could have potentially been worth so much more is instead relegated to the bargain basement instead of Beverly Hills and Rodeo Drive.

Yes, a bit of location, location, and location in the process of attempting to find our true selves at the right place, at the right time, and with the right product. A product that has been created, refined and, I hope perfected, and yet a product with a limited shelf life but paradoxically an unlimited self.

Perhaps that is part of the problem as we buy and sell. The problem so often seems that not only do we not even fully know what we are selling—with all its inner mechanics—but, we don't know our own worth, and we often don't even know our own values.

Did you buy or sell anything today? Do you plan to? I would imagine that, like me, you buy something every day. But what are you selling? What is your product? Right now, my product is—like your product—my self, who I am.

Who am I? Why do I keep asking that question?

This book is another product of mine, a by-product of who I am. Did you buy this product? Was it a gift? What are you buying and what are you selling?

If you are buying, is what you are purchasing a need or a want? Do you want what you need? Do you need what you want? Do you, do I, does anyone? Do we ever—in our buying and selling, in our giving and receiving, in our creating and recreating—really take the time to differentiate between our needs and our wants? And in the process, in the realization, in the epiphany, do we come to know that

119

William Bradford Borden

we have a focused and honest budget, or, instead, a misguided wish list that ultimately creates moral and spiritual deficits? Leaving us searching for a handout, a bailout and a sellout and driving us toward bankruptcy because we never took the time to balance our books and create a vision.

What do you see when you look in the mirror, into the reflection, into the glass? Do you ever take a moment to try to look through someone else's eyes and to imagine what their wants, their needs, their visions might be? Take a moment to think what a snapshot of you—right now, in this moment, and the moment is now—would look like, color or black-and-white, inside or outside' clothed or naked, alone or lonely, happy or sad? What would we see in that snap of a finger, the snap of a shot, the capturing of a moment?

There are the famous nudes of the young Madonna—black-and-white, a bit savage, ripe and wanton—somewhere in N.Y.C. And in my mind I juxtapose them with Vanessa Williams, the current wife of Laker Rick Fox, and I am reminded how of she lost her Miss America title because of her nudes. I wonder, are there nudes of you out there, waiting to be exposed? Or perhaps there is a video—recreating an act—or maybe a still life? Are you embarrassed by your body, of who you are sans costume, sans cover, sans protection; or do you let it all hang out and lustfully expose yourself, all natural? Or perhaps it isn't natural at all but merely plastic, and instead of planting natural seeds and organic growth, you mess with Mother Nature in your implanting.

I do hope that I am not implanting too many ideas and questions, rhetorical and otherwise into your mind. That is not my intent. I guess—and Reagan might have said, and I would agree—I am no Socrates. And perhaps Reagan knew Socrates. I am just attempting to employ the dialogue and to continually ask questions to peel away the layers of the product—yours and mine—in the search for truth.

Where does the search for truth begin; and, in essence isn't truth relative? I would suggest that it begins at home, as a child, with the guidance, and direction (or lack thereof) of parent, parents, or guardians, and I would also concur with Freud. I wonder if he ever wore a slip. And so I have slipped back into banality—please excuse the slip—and does anyone ever wear them anymore? And Freud felt

American Perversity
Sex, Politics and Religion

that the personality was essentially formed in the first five years of our lives.

I just sneezed on the paper, and maybe that is why this blue Intercontinental pen is going on me. Ink is meeting mucus. Yes, I think "Intercontinental" is gone. So I am back to black Pentel R.S.V.P., but "Intercontinental" was significant because it was from the selfsame hotel where I stayed in London at Hyde Park Corner this past Thanksgiving (2002), where I journeyed for my great Aunt Rita's—lovely Rita's—90th birthday celebration.

I have decided that 90 is a good time for my final act; although, I must say, Rita is full of life at 90. My reckoning is that with 90 years I can have five solid acts, in the Shakespearean tradition. Each of the acts would be 18 years. It is almost, from my crunching, a perfect play...

The play—and isn't that what we all desire, to play? It's something we do so much of in our first act, those first 18 years in my case (18 is symbolic because in the Kabalistic tradition 18 represents life; my life will then represent five acts of 18). But then we begin to play less and less, and even though life becomes more of a game, we often savor it less.

Life, I am convinced, is much like the typical drama model and the five-act formula employed by Shakespeare, a fairly good representation of our lives. It is interesting to note, the prior referred to "All's Well That Ends Well" where Shakespeare begins "All the world's a stage..." He then relates his interpretation of life, in the sense of our roles as divided into eight acts, beginning with infant "mewling and puking" and running a complete gamut of school boy, soldier, lover and other progressive roles, and then returning to second childishness.

These eight acts are excellent in delineating our various roles in life, but the five-act drama model that Shakespeare employed for his plays seems more correct in establishing our respective plots and story lines.

In my proposed play of 90 years for example, (which would be four score and 10 years), my five acts will each be 18 years; therefore, I am currently in my third and climatic act. Where are you in your

William Bradford Borden

drama? Have you plotted your course and laid out your play? These are the basics of the five-act model. (My ages are in parenthesis.):

Act I (0-18) is the exposition, when the character, the essence of whom we are and the properties of a soul come to be.

Act II (19-36) is the rising action, when conflict is generated and the roles we are most likely to play are written and assigned. The conflict is essential in testing our mettle and establishing our character, and there are two primary types: interior and exterior. The interior conflicts are all the emotional and psychological soul searching's, while the exterior are all the outer struggles: the physical and financial, natural and man-made.

Act III (36-54) is the climax, where the rising action and all the conflicts have come to head, and the results of all our efforts, our actions and our choices explode in the form or recognition, position and place in society. This can also be the time of midlife crisis.

Act IV (54-72) is the falling action, where resolution is enacted and we begin to come to terms with all conflicts—inner and exterior—and we begin, finally, to appreciate who we are and what we've done and begun. This is also the act where we begin to appreciate our mortality and what impact our lives have made.

Act V (72-90) is the dénouement, a French word for "the end," and this is the act where we begin to wind down and perhaps search even more for ourselves, for spirituality and for self-actualization. It is also a time when we might appreciate our children—and theirs even more—and come to terms that our play is almost over, as we prepare for death and, quite possibly, another script.

Of course, like a heart monitor, our lives go through these dramatic cycles on a daily basis, and the ups and downs replete with conflict, climax and resolution are essential in the play of life. And when they go flat, when the lines are no longer there, then certainly the lights are out and the drama is done.

You might be happy to note that I am done with that section; but what is this section about anyway? Madonna, you might remember, falls into the section on religion but it is right on the line of politics, and she certainly belongs in the sex chapter as well. What chapter would you find yourself in…sex, politics or religion? And for that matter, what act are you immersed in?

American Perversity
Sex, Politics and Religion

Do you ever question where you are in your drama and what role you're playing? Madonna seems content and at peace with where she is and once said, "If I was a girl again, I would like to be like my fans, I would like to be like Madonna."

That is an intriguing thing to say, considering the hardships that Madonna Louise Veronica Ciccone must have endured as a girl. She was born Aug. 16, 1958 (a Leo like J. Lo and there are some remarkable similarities), in Bay City, Michigan outside of Detroit, the current home of Eminem, of whom she is reportedly a fan.

She was the eldest of eight children, according to askmen. com, or six children, according to *People*. Her father, Tony, was a former auto engineer, and her mother, also a "Madonna," was a homemaker. Madonna's mother Madonna died when her daughter Madonna was six, according to askmen. com, or five, according to *People*. It really makes you question asking men, people in general and reporting at all.

Needless to say, Madonna's loss of her mother Madonna to cancer at such an early age must have had a tremendous impact on the budding icon and, perhaps, was the impetus for her need for veneration. Certainly, her mother's life is a perfect example of a different drama model with a different ending...

Madonna attended the highly regarded University of Michigan; the same school that has been so embroiled in highly controversial lawsuits regarding affirmative action. I find this fascinating because the first time I heard her sing she was on *American Bandstand* singing "Holiday," and I was in another room and I loved the song. I was mesmerized as I saw her sing and dance, not only by her awesome talent, but also by the fact that she was white.

At the University of Michigan, she was on a dance scholarship but dropped out after two years and headed for N.Y.C. where she struggled and worked at the counter of Dunkin' Donuts in Times Square. She even joined the world-renowned Alvin Ailey Dance Company, but it seems she was driven for her own unique form of stardom.

In 1983, the same year that Brokaw took over on the Nightly News, Madonna released her first album, which included *Holiday, Borderline*, and *Lucky Star*. The songs became very popular in the

William Bradford Borden

nightclubs and the music videos helped create a fashion sensation that would help to establish the distinctive 80's look.

How are you looking today? Do you have a distinctive look? What do you see when you look in the mirror?

This chapter is thus far my least favorite, and perhaps I reached the climax and I am heading toward the final acts, the falling action and the resolution. I am also questioning the work and am frustrated by my own self-inquisition. Do you do that? Do you question yourself, your worth, and your merit, and in the process sabotage the process? Maybe that is part of the process in and of itself—the inner conflict created by self -doubt and questioning if we can really do it.

How do you do? What do you do? Do you take? The list of do's and don'ts for that matter could go on and on. Do you believe that? Do you make lists? Do you care? I think you get the idea. Don't you?

When I say this chapter is my least favorite it has nothing to do with the subject, and I do hope that it will grow on me, and you, and that I can reach some profound epiphanies and break through all the banalities.

For the 20 years, since 1983—when I was a young Marine and I heard *Holiday* (in the Marine Corps we used to say, "Every day is a holiday, and every meal's a banquet")—until now, May 20, 2003, I have been touched, inspired and impressed by Madonna Louise Veronica Ciccone.

As I mentioned in my J. LO chapter, I have always had a thing for Latin and Italian women, and I'm sure that flame was first lit at 11 or 12 when I first visited Italy and began my love affair with "la dolce vita." There is a soulful, exotic and timeless beauty of Madonna that is both savage and genteel. She is a woman that exudes an aura and appeal that generates its own ray of light.

The more I teach and interact in general, the more I am able to sense and discern people's energies. There is, I believe, in us all, built-in sonar and radar that touch, alert and warn us of our surroundings. It is both a positive and negative system, and if we can sense it in others, they can certainly sense it in us.

Right now a little person walks in and he smiles, he seems happy. I wonder about all his conflicts. I feel sorry for him, and yet I wonder

American Perversity
Sex, Politics and Religion

how he feels for himself. He is less than four feet tall. He must be so strong, and I hear the caffeine pusher call out a "tall mocha" and I look at this 40-something man who could have been me: buzz haircut, grey T-shirt, blue gym shorts, blue and white Jordans, which look like a kid's, very thick calves, sports watch.

I watch. He walks off, walks out, walks away, and I wonder if he feels like the character of Christendom, condemned to walk the ends of earth for eternity. I realize how fortunate I am, but I am still left saddened thinking of his life's plight, and I realize—and I think that I've always somehow known—that we are not all created equal. Yes, there is a form of creation in the actual sexual process, but now much of that process can be created in the laboratory. Life isn't fair. I hope that is a fair assessment.

I feel better now about the direction here because I personally like my meanderings, my weavings and my tangents. I guess I had hoped to economize more and stay more focused and on track—oh well.

How is your well, or your wells? Are you well?

Recently I realized that with my excessive coffee intake, I wasn't consuming enough water. Considering that nearly two-thirds of my body is water, I am much more balanced and healthy when I am massively hydrated.

One of the things I have always appreciated about Madonna is her terrific respect for her body and the way she treats her temple. Of course, not everything is physical, but without a solid physical foundation and good health it is difficult to progress to higher levels of consciousness.

It is well known that Madonna is a big advocate of yoga and the wonders it produces, but in a *USA Today* cover story she relates: "We live in a society that seems to value only physical things, only ephemeral things. People will do anything to get on these reality shows and talent contents on TV. We're obsessed." I wonder if Madonna was once herself in that category, but I so respect her perseverance and artistry. Somewhere, years back, I remember reading that she had a genius level IQ, and I can totally see the brilliance and intellect, although that is something not readily visible, but I'm sure it would be if you were naked...

William Bradford Borden

The '80s was a period when Madonna burst onto the scene and she began to leave a lasting imprint in music and fashion. Do you remember the plethora of crosses, chains and big hair? The '90s was Madonna's more daring period, with the highly graphic coffee-table book *Sex* and her album *Erotica*.

It seems that Madonna has always been comfortable with her body and with nudity. Maybe that is the Mediterranean influence. When I moved to Italy in 1991, after my father's death, I was immediately struck by how sensual and erotic the Italian women were. Topless beaches were the norm and nude beaches quite common.

My first summer there, and for the next two summers, I spent time at the house of a film producer, on the Sicilian island of Stromboli. Stromboli is a group of seven or eight of the Aeolian Islands, and is an active volcano. Ginostra, on the other side of Stromboli, has no cars, no scooters and no electricity. Generators run what minimal electronic devices there are, and donkeys transport supplies. It is an archaic, pristine place that reminds me of Greece, and the 200 to 300 full-time residents are warm and inviting.

It is on Stromboli where I met a then 50-something, well-known sculptress from Milan in the north of Italy. She stayed the whole summer. Her body was chiseled and defined like her art, her skin olive and golden like the land. We met as I walked on huge volcanic rocks along the coast. She was stretched out nude on a big boulder. I asked her what time it was—as if it mattered—and a conversation ensued.

It was the first time that I had seen her alone, and she told me—in fair English—about her time spent at Berkeley, her love for The Doors and for John Irving. She asked me if I wanted to smoke, and I declined as she gracefully crouched behind a rock to shield the wind and fire up her hash pipe. The next day I left the island. Skillfully, she got my number in Rome and a couple of days later the phone rang.

Two weeks later, I met her at a train station in Castello Gandolfo, a seaside resort town in Tuscany, where she had another house. Looking classy, bronzed and blond, she drove me to her house, where

American Perversity
Sex, Politics and Religion

her college-aged daughter was preparing for exams. I slept in the salon.

The next day we went to the beach, and when we returned she asked if I would like a massage on the veranda. I said sure and lay down on a yoga mat, and she straddled me, topless in the afternoon sun, and deeply worked my muscles. Her daughter returned and I felt a bit awkward, but the two said ciao, as if everything was fine, and the "figlia" went inside.

Later in the salon, as I sat across from the daughter as she studied, "Sculpa" (not her real name) smoked hashish in another room. The phone rang and "Figlia" (which means daughter in Italian), went to her bedroom to talk. Sculpa had changed, and now she wore a flimsy, negligee-type get-up that barely covered her round ass. I sat there thinking, as Figlia left the room, and then Sculpa, standing over me to my right, bent down and stuck her tongue down my throat.

I could hear Figlia carrying on a conversation and as we swallowed each others' tongues, sucked each others' juices, and exchanged our breaths. I reached between her muscular thighs with my right hand and felt her warm, moist, dripping sex and wondered what her daughter might think of my index and middle fingers inside her mother, and as Figlia disconnected, so did I.

Later that evening, Figlia went out with her friends and Sculpa and I went out to eat at a local trattoria. I remember the late August evening being very windy, and after dinner we went for a drive in her red compact Fiat. She showed me a camping area frequented by Germans and pulled over to the side of the country road and turned the car off.

She then gave me some headphones, and The Doors were singing as she pulled down her skintight black and floral leotards and proceeded to mount me like Lady Godiva on her stallion. And so we rode, stationary, yet with movement in the Fiat. And afterward, when we went out for ice cream, I realized her pants were on backwards—the tag obviously out. And so we returned to the flat by the sea. I was thirty at the time and not even sure what I was doing with her, and so I went to sleep in the salon, and Sculpa went off to her room.

The next morning, early, before eight, I woke up to Sculpa on her knees by the side of the sofa bed, her mouth on my manhood. And

127

William Bradford Borden

there was this sense of vulnerability and guilt combined with arousal and lust, and I wondered—once again—what would happen if the daughter entered as Sculpa got on top of me and I entered her and thrust into her depths.

I felt, perhaps, what a woman often feels like—violated. Feeling that I had to perform and submit in thanks for the experience of our time together. I cut that trip short and headed back to Rome, after a morning at the beach where I felt, ironically enough, used and abused.

Have you ever felt used and abused and all alone in the world? What is your current perspective or your current state, the state of the union and the state of the world? Have you stated how you felt and voiced your views and opinions, or are you stuck in a state of denial, catatonia or shock?

Again, questions, questions, questions, as I try to move into another day of writing while still dealing with my own general state of mild depression, like a marine layer hovering over the San Fernando Valley. And I am certainly aware that that is a natural cycle—the highs and lows, the ups and downs, and the hills and valleys—and so I drive on and try to do the best I can, and yes, I feel I can.

When I teach my English 101 class, Intro to Composition, I begin by giving them five general techniques for writing essays introductory paragraphs. The first two, *definitions* ("depression is..."), and *direct approach* ("depression in America has increased proportionally with greed"), are discouraged as being too sophomoric (much how this book is feeling these days. Have you noticed how there has not been much erotica lately?). Actually, the other three approaches—the narrative, the background statement, and the rhetorical questions can be explained with erotica.

The "Sculpa Stromboli" story that I just related is a *background statement* because it is something that actually happened. A *narrative* would be (for the intent of differentiation because a narrative can also be factual—but I teach it for introductions as fiction, and that must be confusing as hell) some of my other erotic escapes, like the shower scene or the "mind fuck." The third of the acceptable intro techniques that I employ is the use of *rhetorical questions*, and with them I always encourage the students to ask more than one.

128

American Perversity
Sex, Politics and Religion

All of these last three techniques—the background statements, narrative and rhetorical questions—I have found to be most effective in generating words on paper.

Do you read the paper every day? Which one? I imagine if you're reading this that you read the paper. Have you ever been in the paper? How about a magazine? How much are you worth on paper, and does that worth lose its value when it seems to become a mindless chase? What are you chasing; or rather, are you being chased?

According to the April 28, 2003, *People Magazine*, Madonna's personal fortune is estimated at more than $300 million. What would you do with that kind of money? Madonna relates: "Don't get me wrong. It's fabulous. I have these beautiful homes and paintings, but the most important thing in life is love. I know it sounds corny, but everybody knows it's true."

Yes, I agree with you, Madonna Louise Veronica Ciccone that love is the most important thing in life. But I would have to disagree in that I'm not quite sure, sadly so, that "everybody knows" the power of love. I must say, though, that people like Madonna have helped to spread the message of love through their art and artistry and that's what love—or rather art, or perhaps both—is all about.

Yes, art and love are both about breaking through the banal, the day-to-day and the norm and bringing us to a higher level of transcendence, awakening and passion. That process of making love and making art is quite possibly the only difference between chimpanzees and us. Chimpanzees who share—or maybe it is we that share—99.4 percent of the same DNA...

Part of Madonna's transformation you might attribute to her study of the Kabala—which I also appreciate and revere which asserts that the ancient Hebrew letters are the DNA of the universe. Letters of love maybe...

When I graduated from high school in 1979, my father wrote me the following letter that certainly would concur with Madonna's assertion that "the most important thing in life is love." It took me a long time to realize that, but there is something to be said for a father's wisdom, a father's words, a father's DNA. These are his words...

129

William Bradford Borden

Dear Brad, (June 20, 1979)

Today is graduation day and I am very sad. This is most unfortunate because today is normally a day of happiness, gift giving, family get togethers, all celebrating the achievement of a major goal in our lives.

If all this be true then why am I sad? I am sad for my son who has so much yet realizes so little. A son who is alienated.

Alienated from family. A family who loves him but seemingly cannot reach him. Alienated from his school, a school which has many problems. My son has been one of those problems. Alienated from the system, a system which provides the material things and comforts he enjoys. He fights the system with grand vigor, but to my knowledge he has never won.

Alienated, an alien in his own home.

Yes today is a day of celebration and gift giving. I wish that this day could be a ho-hum type of day like thousands of other families celebrate at graduation time. I wish it were but it isn't.

I give you no material gift. I only give you "Love," but I warn you it is a gift that has no value unless it is shared with your fellow man.

Congratulations on your graduation.

Love, Dad

Even though the loss of my father was absolutely devastating and the ramifications of that loss still ring through my soul, I could not imagine the hurt and pain that Madonna went through when she lost her mother at five or six. What a mother she must be to her children; and what a blessing Madonna has been to me. That's *amore*.

9
Rise Again

After a five-week period of inpatient rehab in Norfolk, Va., in 1983 courtesy of the United States Marine Corps, which literally saved my life, I was compelled to attend regular AA meetings, complete with their 12-step programs. I say that the rehab literally saved my life because a year or so earlier I had dropped out of college, given up on the Army ROTC and becoming an officer, because I was sure that Israel's incursion into Lebanon—and then the Marines joining them—was the beginning of something big, possibly the end, and I wanted to be a part of it.

My gunnery sergeant was in contact with my father and both of them thought I was crazy, which I'm sure I was (and probably still am), but I was doing all I could. That was why I had joined, to go and fight. I was definitely fighting and drinking, letting the rage fly at will, and after several incidents I was evaluated and scheduled to go to be healed, to be rehabilitated, to be "saved." Approximately 10 days after I arrived in Norfolk for treatment, the building in Beirut where I might have been was suicide-bombed and more than 260 Marines were killed. Maybe there is something to be said for Divine Intervention.

Maybe, instead, there is something to be said for being in the right place at the right time, which ultimately was the result of a series of choices, many in my control and many not. After rehab, I went back

131

William Bradford Borden

to El Toro, Calif., and then, less than a year later, I was shipped off to Iwakuni, Japan, on the mainland on the southern tip, about 40 miles south of Hiroshima.

My first year in Japan I met Miyuki, who would become my lover, my friend, and my mate. At the same time I got very tired of the same-old-same old at the only AA meeting on the base, and so I stopped attending, and instead went to a Bible study that would end up dramatically altering the course of my life.

A Marine captain who literally had "Christ" in his name headed the "study." A good name, one would think, for leading a study of the Bible. He was about 5'5", stocky and formidable, with a gravelly voice, and green-inked tattoos on his forearms that were faded from the years and obscured by considerable hair. When he spoke, I listened, and I became consumed by the message. I became an adherent, a follower and a sheep. I guess I had forgotten about the "wolves' clothing" thing.

This is all so difficult to write about because in retrospect it all seems so foolish and misguided, but then, I imagine, most of us do those kinds of things throughout our lives that we later regret. To dwell on them makes no sense to me. Certainly there is something to be said for learning from our mistakes. Anyway, I became a born-again Christian, which today strikes me as absurd, considering I grew up Episcopalian and my family was very involved with the church.

I think that of the three—sex, politics and religion—the discussion of religion leaves me most disgusted, nauseated and perplexed. To give you an idea of the scope of my "devotion," it was "made in Japan" and lasted from 1985-1987 and beyond...

I broke up with Miyuki, and remained celibate for more than two years—completely celibate. There was no swimming with members of the opposite sex, church three times a week, evangelism, no movies, and I would fast for three days straight each month.

Just recounting all of this seems utterly foolish, absurd and misdirected—as though there were huge holes in my perceived holiness. Certainly Marx had it right, and the former escapes of sex, drugs and rock-and-roll were replaced by religion, truly an "opiate for the masses." It was intoxicating, deceiving and ultimately empty because there was no moderation, no tolerance and no compassion.

American Perversity
Sex, Politics and Religion

The hole had been filled with self-righteousness, condemnation and alienation.

After Capt. "Christ" left, the pastor from Pittsburgh arrived. He was on fire, and he spoke of his time at a Bible College in Charlotte, N.C., where I now (and now was in 1987) felt compelled to attend. I felt called, I felt chosen, and I felt lost. When I returned to New Jersey, I further alienated my family by letting them know that they weren't going to "make it" with their "liberal" Episcopal Church, and I proceeded to be the biggest hypocrite imaginable.

Imagination is probably what I most was lacking at the time because I was so blinded by what I now perceive as not only an opium haze but also a grand illusion to the literary allusion of the biblical text. The biblical text, I have come to realize is full of songs, poetry, prose, genealogy, and dream interpretations. "Interpretation" is the operative word, which, in essence is why there are so many denominations. Yes, when I now look at it with maturity, wisdom and experience, I realize the absurdity of it all.

Shabbat Shalom! It is the Sabbath and I am back in San Diego at the Starbucks here, and here I hear much of the same—coffee machines, chatter and background music. I do not hear much silence and I ask myself how many of the caffeine junkies prayed this morning? How many of them, before they ventured out, said a little prayer? I wonder how many of them believe in prayer.

What are prayers anyway? Are they just configurations of words and thoughts that are recited in unison with no connection to their very connotation? Does prayer instead become the idle recitation of denotative words that might not even be known to the reader? Or, perhaps, prayer is a plea, a cry for help at the last moment, when the possibility for change and transformation is a moment too late. And yet, I know from various surveys that the majority of Americans believe in God and the power of speaking words in supplication.

Right now, my sister, the high-powered $1 million-plus per year securities lawyer sits to my left and reads the Madonna chapter, and I wonder what she thinks. She doesn't praise easily and, in fact, probably prays less, and so I will value her opinion, but I imagine it will be critical, and that will probably only serve to strengthen my resolve to get it right. Looking at her body language and realizing her

William Bradford Borden

lack of praise, neither bodes well for her criticism, and yet that is okay considering the lack of praise in her life and that there are so many people like her. People who are rewarded with enormous financial sums, seemingly beautiful homes and exquisite clothes, and yet there is a poverty of joy, a deficit of sunshine, and a bankruptcy of hope.

What do you hope for as you bob for an apple to place on the desk? Is your desk organized and focused or cluttered like your mind? Do you eat an apple a day and get regular dental checkups? Do you go through life without a plan…(and now she says to me, "I didn't know Dad wrote you that letter," and I nod my head, and she adds, "Dad was a great man," as I continue to write, hoping and praying as the synapses ignite, muscles move and pen scratches, that his DNA has etched me and that I can at least be good as I seek the goodness in the world) and I do have a plan, but do you? Do you care about how things turn out or leave it all to fate, choice and destiny or, instead, get down on your knees and think of things to say, all in the hope of a prayer. My sister places the chapter on my Franklin Day Planner, saying nothing as the pen fades…

Pen fades out and gone now, no comment, and then a minute or so later she asks, "How long have you been writing?" and I say, "A couple of months," and she asks what motivated the writing and I don't respond and she asks, "What's the focus?" and I respond, after a long, contemplative pause, that the focus is finding the focus, and she says it has lots of themes, and I agree…She goes to the bathroom, returns, and asks…

"Do you think you have mood swings…?" And so the chapter did make her question something, and then she relates something about her friend's daughter, whose psychologist thinks, might have mood swings as she gets older…

Do you see, feel and understand that you are getting older or are you stuck in some sort of Dick Clark time warp? What would a timeline with all the significant people, places and things look like if your life were charted?

I was thinking about that yesterday, after my sister had read the prior chapter, and I contemplated all the choices and decisions that led me to the various places, where I encountered the various people and

American Perversity
Sex, Politics and Religion

where I did the various things. The concept, previously discussed, of the six degrees of separation was also contemplated.

My timeline, in a linear, written sense, would read something like this in regards to place and time.

1961	* Born in Kansas City, Missouri
1964-1979	* New Jersey
	Numerous trips to Europe: England, France, Greece, Italy, Portugal, Spain, Portugal, Greece. Mexico and Argentina
1979	* January-June Downtown YMCA Phoenix, Arizona
1979	* June-August returned to New Jersey
1979-1982	* Arizona State University Tempe, Arizona
1983-1985	* Marine Corps Air Base, El Toro, California
1985-1987	* Marine Corps Air Base, Iwakuni, Japan
	Two deployments to Korea; one to the Philippines
1987	* January-April returned to New Jersey
1987-1991	* University of North Carolina at Charlotte, Deployments to Israel, Belize and Florida with North Carolina Air National Guard
	Studied Shakespeare in Stratford and London
1991-1993	* Rome, Italy
1993-1997	* Studio City, California
1997-2002	* Encino, California
2003-Present	* Studio City, California

What would your timeline look like? How do you mark your highs and lows? If I have decided on 90 for my final act, then my timeline would end at 2051. Location, location, location, and basic math, all adding up to a virtual scorecard of life that won't be found on the Sports page but the Obituaries—that is always a profound

135

William Bradford Borden

writing assignment, to have students write their own obituaries—what would you say, what would you want people to know; do you even care?

Today is Memorial Day and many Americans do not even appreciate the significance—how sad. To my right are six Los Angeles firemen, sitting at a table they have now installed for handicapped people. There is laughter. I hear something about high heels and, a moment earlier, a 60-something New York woman complimented them on their cool T-shirts and asked if they sold them in boutiques and then something about how she lives near Ground Zero.

In essence, Ground Zero has become the site of a perpetual Memorial Day—a day to remember the people who have given their lives in sacrifice for America. Typically, it is to honor the war dead, the soldiers. But that is what the New York City firemen and policemen became—soldiers on the front lines—and I would imagine a large percentage of them had military service. And so I know the Los Angeles Fire Department is ready to go, as inevitably this "war"—and I don't even know why I put it in quotation marks, because it is a war, real or perceived.

I think of Ground Zero and the concept of marking a spot with a number, with zero, with nothingness; but the zero also seems like the bull's eye, the objective, the center of the target, and I think, "What are our opportunities? What are our choices? How many more memorials will be necessary to find some compromise, some rationality, some hope, or is the whole concept of justice, of peace, of harmony, just a wish and a prayer?"

And prayers will be said for the dead, but what about the living, those that utter the prayers? I wonder if they appreciate the greatness, the possibility, and the wonder of America or have our prayers become empty, mechanical and hopeless?

United we stand and sit, and kneel, maybe. Perhaps not, but have we taken the time—and time is of the essence—to say thank you to the Veterans of World War II, those christened the Greatest Generation. And today is Memorial Day, a Monday, the 26th of May. There was once a fixed date for Memorial Day, like the Fourth of July. Like the Fourth of July, Memorial Day celebrates our war

136

American Perversity
Sex, Politics and Religion

culture, our war industry, and our power—a culture that has a by-product of dead, who we venerate, and honor. But instead of really giving thanks for the ultimate sacrifice, instead of true respect and dedication we shift the day to a Monday so we can have a three-day-weekend to "unofficially" begin the summer.

And so begins another cycle of the passage of time, of the seasons, creating the contrasts and rhythms of work and play, sowing and reaping, war and peace, as the Veterans of World War II leave us at a rate of more that a thousand a day. I would love to know their thoughts, their prayers and their hopes on this Memorial Day. I would love to see their timelines, hear their stories, and read their obituaries. I would love to say thank you.

I think it is fairly significant that in this first chapter in the section on religion, chapter 9 of 10, I still have not mentioned the subject source. I am okay with that, in that by the table of contents or chapter title you know who it is about and I guess in most of the chapters the focus has not really been the matter. Maybe there was credence in my response to my sister when she asked what the focus of the book was and I responded that the focus was finding the focus. Maybe there was, and is, tremendous truth in that—in my search for what America is all about. All about I go looking for truth and justice and the American way. Right, sure, I think that comes from some superhero concept.

How does the concept of religion—organized or not—strike you? Have you been struck by the hand of God? Or do you continue to strike out at your family, yourself, your country, in the hope of striking a balance?

Again I am questioned by direction as my stomach turns, as 10 minutes before I felt a hand on my back and it was Vivian, the Vivian who has meant so much to me the last three years. The Vivian who reminds me so much of my mother and sister; the Vivian who was my former student who wrote me the touching letter that hangs on my wall; the Vivian who designed my place; the Vivian with blue-green eyes who looks like Catherine Zeta Jones; the Vivian who now sits outside the Starbucks with a boy named Chris, at a table where I often write, our backs are back-to-back; the Vivian who said she got my

William Bradford Borden

message—thank you; the Vivian who her friend's mother just said to me smiling, "Oh, I see who you're flirting with."

The Vivian who I cut myself off from because I didn't want that perception, the Vivian who is now 21, but whose soul is timeless; the Vivian who for the last three years I went to movies with and ate sushi with; the Vivian whom I took to the opera; the Vivian who made me laugh; the Vivian who helped open my heart and touch my soul; the Vivian I thought of last night when I told the naked gal on my bed I didn't want a "fuck buddy," that I wanted to make love; the Vivian that I respect and honor more than almost anyone; the Vivian that I would love to be the mother of a William Borden.

The Vivian who loves to read and discuss; the Vivian who could have been a movie star; the Vivian who decided to help people instead; the Vivian who helped me believe in the God of Israel; the Vivian who reminds me that there is still good in the world; the Vivian I haven't seen for fifty days; the Vivian who always challenges me and gives me hope; the Vivian who on the last Sabbath day I saw her, on the fifth of April, I held in my arms and, later, in front of a delusional doctor, said she's probably the only woman I could ever marry, and I meant it.

The Vivian who will always be 21 years younger, but 21 years older as well; the Vivian who, if there wasn't a window, I could lean back and the backs of our heads would touch; the Vivian that I feel through the glass anyway, the Vivian who is first-class and should always be treated as such; the Vivian who has taught me more than she'll ever know; the Vivian who I love, who I always have and always will; the Vivian of my prayers, and this is my prayer for Vivian, that she knows that she has been such a radiant light, such a wise soul, and such a blessing to me, to America, and the world—that is my prayer for Vivian.

"I think therefore I am." You may remember the earlier Descartes reference, and once again, a less-than commendable segue, but not everything in life deserves commendation, and so I just attempt—hours later on this Memorial Day weekend—to get something down, and what I was thinking when I began this paragraph was that I would insert Vivian's letter—the one that hangs framed on my wall:

American Perversity
Sex, Politics and Religion

Borden,   6-19-00

Graduation is in less than four days. And since you decided you didn't want to attend, I decided to write you a letter on everything I would want to tell you as a graduate (so my grade would not be affected).

I feel like you have been my teacher for all four years, rather then one very long year. I feel like we have gone through so much together. Although I can't say I have learned the type of knowledge that will be helpful in my college classes, from you I have learned a lot about people and the male way of thinking. You are the type of guy that parents try to keep from their virginal daughters. Maybe that's why so many women are attracted to you, because they know you are bad.

Although we had many conflicts in class, and I was never afraid to speak my mind to you, I really do respect you, maybe not as a teacher, but as a friend. You have a very sweet core to your personality, but I think you're scared to show it. You hide under this mask, out of fear of being hurt...

I didn't write this letter to analyze your personality, but to tell you that you mean a lot to me and that you made my senior year special and memorable, not to mention stressful. I wish you much love and happiness in life. Enjoy life after Grant.

Love always, Vivian

The letter is itself a prayer and so I will let it speak for itself. It would be nice if we wrote our own prayers, scripted our own lives and created our own possibilities; for certainly there is extraordinary power in words, in ideas, in prayer.

So, back to my timeline, to transitions, from Japan to New Jersey, and it was back in "The Garden State" where I left off pages ago after returning from the "Land of the Rising Sun," and if you will remember I had returned as a born-again, self-righteous sheep that had forgotten the power of the very God that lay within me. Without

William Bradford Borden

that essence of a freethinking individual, what was supposed to be found in being "born-again" was sadly for me paradoxically still lost.

"Why is this timeline important?" you may wonder and I think its relevance lies in the various choices and decisions—"free will"—if you will, that led me to where I am today. "Who is leading you?" I ask. Are you a leader or a follower? Perhaps you play Follow-the-Leader with someone who willingly leads you astray, or maybe the leader plays a different way, or quite possibly, maybe you should have been the leader in the first place, but sheepishly you acquiesced your power, and as the hour moves closer to midnight you realize the shell game as you are given the menu with a main course of mutton with lily liver, and as the clock strikes midnight the dessert of pumpkin pie is presented as you look outside and your chariot is a fire.

Transitioning out of the Marine Corps and back to civilian life in New Jersey was transitional in and of itself, but going to the Reserves was helpful. I joined a Marine Reserve unit in Red Bank, but I knew I had to get out of New Jersey, out of the house I had left when I was 17. The road was calling.

I felt called to preach the Gospel. I had been enamored with Jimmy Swaggart and his preaching and believed it was my destiny to go to the Bible College in North Carolina. Yet, I also knew that I needed to finish my degree, so I headed back west to Arizona to finish my last semester, and to a strong job possibility my dad had arranged catering on airplanes at Sky Harbor Airport in Phoenix.

I had bought an old 1965 blue Dodge truck with a shift on the column, and even though the truck was 22 at the time, she was solid, powerful, and comfortable. I then got one of those big camper shells that you place inside the bed of the truck and bolt down. A queen bed actually rested on the cab of the truck. I filled up the Dodge with all my possessions: books, clothes, music, some furniture, and I even attached a motorcycle I had brought back from Japan to the front bumper. I headed west even though I still felt called south. After several months at "home" the road was ready, I was too, and my family was most certainly glad that I was gone.

Before I left, I had to buy a spare tire and I was told at the junkyard that the Ford rim would work fine. By the time I reached St.

140

American Perversity
Sex, Politics and Religion

Louis, close to midnight, the passenger side rear tire blew out and I somehow, miraculously, changed it as massive rigs whizzed by an arm's length away. Thankfully, I had also brought an industrial-sized jack that rolled under the truck—much like the ones used in NASCAR.

A day or so before St. Louis, I had stopped in Columbus, Ohio, where I visited my relatives. And so I was now on to Oklahoma City, to visit my then 80-something grandfather, the retired University of Oklahoma professor who fluently spoke more then 10 languages and was a true scholar. After staying a night at his Bruce Goff home (a contemporary Frank Lloyd Wright) we said our goodbyes, and after a nice laugh, off I headed west again. On the 10, Interstate 10 to Phoenix, and the phoenix rose...

Yes, out of Phoenix rose my future, my opportunity and possibility, and yet I wasn't very excited to be returning to the desert where I had struggled so. Still, I knew it was important to finish my degree and all of these things were on my mind as I cruised at a steady 75 mph.

In Oklahoma, like much of the middle of America, the topographic features are rather limited and the terrain generally flat— much like this writing which again seems stilted as I progress foot by foot, mile by mile, year by year, in my timeline of fate, chance and choice, and I was enjoying the drive, albeit it was a bit boring, but I was closer to my goal and I felt the tires, even without a spare, would get me there.

What happened next is etched in my mind in slow motion, and in today's speeds, 75 mph is slow, but all of a sudden—and I find it surreal that "all" can literally happen in a sudden moment—I lost control of the machine, a machine that had been created, built and sold by men and I, at 26, was supposed to be the master.

I was supposed to be in control. I was supposed to be in charge and suddenly that changed as the rear Ford rim on the '65 Dodge, two different creations, from two different creators, sheared off the lug nuts that held the rim to the axle and literally cut itself, sheared itself, amputated itself like a major decision with life and death in the balance, and the very act of balancing the truck on the remaining three tires became impossible.

141

William Bradford Borden

Somehow, miraculously maybe, I wove from the fast lane, three lanes over to the large, grassy side of the road, where the camper became disengaged and crumbled as it flew. The motorcycle in front also detached but somehow the truck didn't roll. The people came, stopped and surveyed the area: books and clothes strewn, camper on top of motorcycle, truck with three tires. It looked like a disaster, natural and man-made. I knew better, for I "knew" it was the hand of God. I was going the wrong way.

You've got to hand it to God, and it wasn't even a proverbial fork in the road, nor a road less traveled, or anything to do with diverging. What was it then? Then is what it was and once again it's a matter of semantics and wordplay and perhaps swordplay as I remind you once again that the pen is...

So there I was on the side of the road and the "Okies" stopped, and they were generous and kind, and they thought it was a miracle, but I knew better and I wasn't a gambler, so I gathered my belongings in the back of the bed, got towed to some mechanic's shop in the rural town 50 miles or so outside of Norman, Okla. got the rim repaired, called my grandfather and told him I was turning around. And so I went from the Far East to the East Coast, to heading west like a good young man to a transformational 180-degree turn—half a circle in the game of life to a new destination, new coordinate, a place I felt had been plotted by a master planner.

When I arrived in Charlotte, N.C., I immediately checked out the bible college, the tongue-speaking, evangelical, ultraconservative organization where I was going to study the Word of God and become a good, old-fashioned preacher. The irony was that I was blind and couldn't see the hypocrisy until the game revealed itself and the dominoes began to fall. Jimmy Swaggart was caught with a prostitute and tearfully asked forgiveness from his enablers. Jim Baker and his wife Tammy, just south of the border with their tears, mascara and greed were exposed and the passing the loot (and lute?) revealed. And the final blow—with my strict adherence to the tenants of deception with my more then two years of celibacy—I found out that it appeared many of the "mighty" 200 strong student body were fornicating like Lot, or rather in the parking lot, but still, perhaps a lot.

American Perversity
Sex, Politics and Religion

I realized the hypocrisy, feeling like such a fool, but a miracle had happened and no longer blind, I could see.

When I was newly enlightened, I felt liberated and I was excited as I signed up for classes at the University of North Carolina, at Charlotte. I liked Charlotte and the genuine Southern hospitality, and my first semester I audited a women's studies class that met once a week. The first week we sat in a circle, and in a class of 20 or so, I was the only male. I was 27 now and across from me was a tall, sexy blonde, and I was immediately drawn to her. The second week, the class went to the library and I spoke with the 18-year-old "Sinead." She was bright, engaging, and charming. The third week, she moved in with me in a mobile home, which I had bought near the Bible College, behind the Copal Grill, a mile from the airport, in the Hunter Mobile Home Park.

A hunter I had become again, no longer a sheep, I had found my prey, and for almost nine months we lived together, and in retrospect I wished we might have prayed together because in many respects there was so much to be said for the two of us, and yet, like so often, you don't realize how good something is until it's gone. That is another story, a North Carolina story to be sure, but now is the time to finally introduce the other North Carolina story, the tribute of this chapter, and I would love to know his opinion of my scriptures. I'm sure it would be labeled blasphemous, evil, and of the devil, and to that I would say if a man had ideas and opinions of his own and was willing to discuss them rationally and logically, then a man would still be a man, but a group of men couldn't be "a men," so I guess there will probably be no amens. Can't I get an amen? Don't I even have a prayer? Don't you? I bet you do, and I'm no bettor, but you better, and everyone said "Amen, amen...

This North Carolina story is a tribute then, and I think that this chapter, 9 of 10, sets the record, for getting to the point slowest, and what is the focus of the book again? Where is all of this heading? The focus is finding the focus and perhaps establishing a vision for an America, questing for answers amongst all the sex, politics, and religion.

As this blue pen—Mr. Good, BH-591, 0.5 Korea—begins to fade, I can at least let you know that this is, in essence, a North Carolina

William Bradford Borden

story, and it is dedicated to William Franklin Graham, Jr. who was born near Charlotte, North Carolina, Nov. 7, 1918, a Scorpio. I wonder if "Billy" is an astrology buff.

Once again the degrees of separation are closer than imagined, as "Mr. Good," born in Korea drips its last drop of fluid, and so this pen is, no longer—fading away, a creation like most, mortal in the end. But there is hope for an afterlife, and so, perhaps I will give it a chance for another life, for reincarnation, for 72 ink pen virgins, as I look for a place to recycle the martyr. And around it all goes, some lives measured in circles, others in straight lines.

The line then between the proverbial point A and point B is not always straight, nor narrow is the path; although, we have often been told that the quickest and most expeditious way to move from two points is in a straight line. Often, this is not feasible, not desired and quite possibly not possible. We plot our courses and on our ways there is discourse, intercourse, and sometimes no recourse as we coordinate our coordinates, some of us using terrain features, others a compass, and still others Global Positioning Satellites, as I transition into Wednesday, to hump day, to the first day of the rest of my life, and I feel rejuvenated and well-rested after my first night with an herbal stress reliever, Valerian root. I want to shout out, I want to cheer, I want to be corny—I'm rooting for you!

The new day also brings a new pen—now that Mr. *Good, BH-591, 0.5 Korea* has lost his mojo and that pen is no longer capable of ejaculating. Hard yes, but its tubes have been tied so I move on to this black *Pilot Easy Touch Med*, and I hope and pray that the "Pilot" is well-trained, knows the way and can lead me to the desired destination, perhaps higher ground as I attempt to chart a course...

The tone here seems to me—and do you hear the tones or are you tone deaf? —sarcastic and it probably is, and to that I apologize because I realize sarcasm can run thin, like a shroud on a mummy in a sarcophagus, the sarcasm becomes deadly in its execution as the tone rings out like a funeral dirge and in the wake...

In the wake...I awaken to the stunning beauty that sits four feet away. She opens *Summer Travel* and now a magazine called *Vacations*. She pulls a silver phone with headset out of her white jeans, "YMI" on the brown label on her waist. Her olive skin

144

American Perversity
Sex, Politics and Religion

gracefully pours out; her tight gray shirt exposes her mid-drift. Her breasts are real, and full—full C's—and she just turned to look at me and there is contact, deep blue eyes, an anomaly with her black hair and olive skin. Her watch is on her right wrist—probably a lefty and she sneezed and I said, "Bless you," and she is a blessing, a godsend. And what an experience it would be to get down on my knees before her and worship her, to bow down before this goddess and with my lips, praise her and whisper into her soul, and give thanks for the splendor and joy and that which is divine, that which is woman, that which is God-given.

And the name of this goddess is Kati and we have spoken and I am honored to have spoken with this wonder woman, who I now know is Kurdish and she recounts a bit of her life as I quest to know her. She speaks through the fullest of chartreuse lips—which I imagine mirror the lips that will one day bring forth life—and I am left in awe.

There is so much to worship, so much to praise in Kat, the businesswoman who owns gas stations. She talks on her phone about a gas delivery and the Fritos driver, and then says a few things in an ancient language and hangs up. She is Muslim, but not Arab. She is Kurdish, but also Aryan. And there will be a race for many to get to that line, to start and finish...

And the lines she must hear, but she doesn't need to recite them like some parrot, for she writes her own, scripting her life and getting ready to move to Miami, and I give her my card and want to share with her the praise and adoration.

"Bless you" were my first words to her, to Kati, which is pronounced like "cot" and "tea," with the accent on tea. Yes, after she sneezed, her breath of life and I blessed her, I asked her to watch my journal and when she acknowledged me—the one who would be her humble servant, her slave, ready to serve her—when I looked into the depths of her soul and told her she was stunning, and I could have been less cunning but the "lingus" on her juicy lips would be a gift of the gods.

She drinks Plum Delicious Tazo, and that is what Kati is, "plum delicious," I'm certain, and the fruits of her juices pour out an aroma and there is no poverty here. No, here there is a wealth of riches far

William Bradford Borden

grander than one can imagine and the imagination is what is left desiring, wanting to know how someone so blessed can be so humble, can be so kind, can be so exotic. She's the kind that would make a wonderful mother, producing extraordinary children and guiding them right, but she is also a woman who knows her power, who knows her magic, who knows her self, and the self is timeless.

And as she looks at her self wearing nothing but a smile, her womanhood exposed, she knows God has been kind and she returns the kindness to the world, for at her center is the knowledge of the truth behind the chicken and the egg. As the cock crows and she readies to go, and I hold her hand, look her in the eye, tell her that I wrote her two more pages, and "it was so nice meeting you," and as I hold her hand, together we're one, as I say "God bless you."

As I finish writing that, she is gone now more than a minute, and now I literally give one of my last dollars to a Hispanic man who is almost completely native, a real American, dark and small. Our hands touch in another prayer as I hand him the green paper. That is life: worship, adoration and prayer.

In the Sat., May 3, 2003, *Los Angeles Times,* there is a large black-and-white photo of the right Rev. Billy Graham. It is an almost perfect headshot in the horizontal, but he doesn't need to submit his picture like the thousands and thousands of other actors in Los Angeles. He has already landed the part, the job, and the role as America's emissary to God. Perhaps he knows somebody. He certainly has connections and, more importantly, a gift for connecting. He has a remarkable stage presence, leading-man looks, and Shakespearean voice.

The bold headlines, beneath the headshot proclaim "Faithful are expected to flock to evangelist's San Diego visit" and then, beneath the headline, a sub headline—and it seems sublime—reads, "Many followers of the Reverend Billy Graham believe health problems and age may make next week's mission event his last appearance in area." Beneath that the byline reads "By Steve Hymon" and then the article begins, "The praying won't stop until something happens."

And then Hymon continues in the next paragraph with an explanation: "That's the slogan for 'Mission San Diego', which is

146

American Perversity
Sex, Politics and Religion

expected to draw 200,000-plus Christians next week to hear the Reverend Billy Graham."

The root of the word "reverend" is "revere," and often I feel the reverence to man—men of God maybe, but often the greater reverence to them than the God they serve—often seems the root of so many of the problems facing religions across the spectrum. Yet notwithstanding Graham's admitted anti-Semitic musings with another of our "great" presidents, Richard Nixon, decades past, which we certainly can and should forgive. Should we forget? Do we ever really forget?

But again, I find such hypocrisy—not with Graham, who seems to deserve the title "Reverend," who seems to be truly a man of God, and actually does seem anointed—with the Religious Right, who much like Graham didn't want anything to do with the Jews, didn't want them in their neighborhoods, their schools or their country clubs, yet now they want to embrace them, to embrace Israel and the Jews.

Perhaps they realize that it was the Romans who killed Christ, not the Jews, and the hypocrisy continues as the Right attempts to right and perhaps also write all the wrongs in order to make their biblical prophecy come to with fruition. But what is left is an ultraconservative coalition that doesn't believe in gun control, abortion, or mitzvahs. This is in stark contrast with a group of "chosen" that do. They are the strangest of bedfellows, Evangelical and Jew, right and left, conservative and liberal. A relationship sadly, in some ways, representing that of pimp and prostitute, choosy and chosen, wrong and right.

The article continues:

"Because of health problems and age, many followers believe the mission will be the last time the fiery 84-year-old preacher appears in Southern California, where his evangelical career began."

At the bottom of the article is a picture of Graham in 1949, at the age of 31, and his lips are snarled back like Mick Jagger and his strong white teeth are exposed, his arms open wide, his fists clenched with the index finger of each hand pointed out and up and the caption reads, "The Reverend Graham delivers a sermon to a crowd on a downtown street corner in Los Angeles in 1949."

147

William Bradford Borden

Seven miles to the west of Studio City is Encino. I still have properties there, and so I also feel part of that community. It is markedly different from Studio City. But I also hear a script being pitched, something about an omen, and trees sticking through people, and from a distance I hear the three men and one says, "So what's our first step?"

To my right there are two different tables with Middle Eastern men and surely they have long traditions of coffee houses. They play chess, contemplating each other's moves, and the observers contemplating theirs much like war, and the seven miles is a world apart. Though further west than Studio City, Encino is farther east in its ethnic composition, with a very large and proud Persian population. Their women, these Persian princesses, a proportional mix of Muslim and Jew, are so often supremely sensual, feminine and exotic. They know their power and their place and they let you know that they know that you know they know and that knowledge is priceless.

And in Los Angeles rarely does one ask how far it is to get from place to place but instead in Los Angeles we ask how long does it take, and so we return again to give and take. And there are so many corners in Los Angeles, though minutes and miles from home, that even the most anointed and charismatic person wouldn't stand and preach as the mass of humanity drives by, driving by, driving on, driven to get to our various destinations and praying for miracles.

Do you believe in miracles and in the mighty hand of God parting the Red Sea, or allowing one who was blind to see? Or saving Private Lynch, which it turns out, might not have been the miracle that the people in Palestine (West Virginia, that is) thought it was? Instead— like the parting of water at Universal Studios—the miracle is in magic and in smoke and mirrors, and if you really do believe in miracles, then why do so many bad things happen to so many seemingly good people?

I know there's a best-selling book out about that, but then why is evil so often rewarded with yachts and palaces and jewels, as the opiated masses, looking for their miracles, for their deliverance, their transformation, idle along in neutral? And yes, I asked some of these

American Perversity
Sex, Politics and Religion

questions earlier, but I want an answer now, and you can tell me, because we're talking about religion, but what about spirituality?

Yes, you can tell me that there will be rewards in "glory," but why is it that so many of your reverends, your mullahs, and your rabbi's, why is that they are constantly saying things like, "Judge not lest you be judged," and "Do unto others..." yet they seem to be the very ones living in the glass houses, driving the fancy chariots and wearing the Italian suits?

Maybe you're not wearing Italian suits, okay, I'll give you that, maybe instead you're wearing some bizarre robe that you had an altar boy help you into as you helped yourself into him. Or maybe you're wearing some full-length robe and then forcing your women to completely hide themselves in a cloth tent prison. Or maybe you wear some 17th century Eastern European black-get-up that, for a religion which is almost 5000 years old, seems to make absolutely no fashion sense.

Does any of this make sense? Does it suit you? Are we—am I—finding my focus? I am definitely not giving you much of a picture of my chosen ten, but instead of looking for a bit of heaven on earth, trying to question many universally accepted concepts and ideas, and I don't need a studio or a stage, not even a street corner, just a piece of paper and a pen. As I mentioned earlier, I took up another pen and this pen, began its reign when I paid tribute to Kati.

What if she was God? What if God was a woman? What if she were a Kurdish, Sagittarian Muslim living in Studio City? What if I praised her, on paper, this morning with a pen, and a prayer? Maybe it really is all right there. Maybe it really is simply black and white...

150

10
America

I am almost certain that this 10th chapter, this final chapter in ten, a minion of ideas representing more of a concept and a group than an individual, and so for that reason I have "created" an acronym to represent those of the twelve tribes of Israel, the chosen, the Jews. I have designated "AMERICA," to represent: Art and Advertising, Medicine, Entertainment, Religion, Industry, Clothing, and Authors.

I already feel strained and constrained because I greatly appreciate the gravity, magnitude and significance of the potential interpretations, misinterpretations and reinterpretations of my conceptions, misconceptions and perceptions.

Much like Genesis, the Old Testament Book of the Jews, this chapter will be a lot of lists, representative samples of America. And it really is not an acronym in the truest sense of the word, in that the word "America" already represents North, South, and Central, as well as the United States of ... Instead, "America" serves as a mnemonic device to show the power and the prestige of this statistically miniscule group (and I was going to write race, but the Jews are not a race) of people with massive influence in America and the world.

There are, of course, other areas where this band of brothers and sisters wield substantial power, but for the sake of an argument—and wouldn't you agree that everyone loves one—I will just let AMERICA represent America. It is all of our destinies—yours and

151

William Bradford Borden

mine—and yet, theirs is an ancient story recorded in the black box of time.

I will jump a bit to the center of America, to the "R," Middle America where religion reigns supreme, but the supremacy is not supreme. And because the middle of America is a bit thick, the belt is tightened and family Bibles are passed from generation to generation. If there are few Jews in America and the world, there are even a fewer here, in the wheat-and corn-fed middle, for the Jews are more likely to be found on the coasts in places like New York and Los Angeles, as well as Miami and Chicago.

Traditionally New York City and Los Angeles with their large Jewish populations, tend to be more liberal and democratic and to the left than those in the center. In the Bible belt and the South, the tendency is much more conservative, republican and right. Does that contrast, that difference, and that doctrine make one right and one wrong? Does it create conflict and polarization, or are these differences in America necessary to create balance?

An amazing irony, at least from my perspective…

My perspective has shifted to Friday, the 30th of May 2003, the true Memorial Day, as opposed to an arbitrary Monday that shifts each year in deference to a three-day weekend—72-hour defection from work for the majority of Americans. Yes, it is—or rather it has become, these Memorial Day Mondays—less memorable and more arbitrary.

For observant Jews, Friday evening is never arbitrary, and so perhaps this Memorial Day is special for me because as a semi-observant "goy" I honor the Sabbath. I honor the Shabbat. I honor those who have given their lives. And as evening sets in I reflect upon those who made the ultimate sacrifice.

The sun gently lowers, inch-by-inch, light-year-by-light-year, readying itself—the perfect full-circle to melt over Malibu and dip into the Pacific—swimming toward Pearl Harbor to the ultimate resting place for the ultimate sacrifice, the eternal Shabbat. Marking the spot for so many, in Hawaii, and Arlington and Normandy, holding the ground, in formation, with military precision, left right left, rows and rows, column after column.

American Perversity
Sex, Politics and Religion

Soldiers, sailors, airmen and Marines…in squads and platoons, companies and battalions, brigades and corps, divisions and armies all in white, with their arms extended outward, erect and straight they stand, forever in formation. Crosses symbolizing a father, a son, a holy ghost—up and down, over and across, representing crisis, the crosses proclaiming supplication to a prophet, a messenger, a Jew—a Jew who had his own title, for what he was fighting for. This was the Prince of Peace…

Yes, indeed the "R" in America, for my argument, stands for religion. And the Jewish religion has had a much more profound impact on the United States than one might imagine. It is the imagination of the Jews, maybe—the great arbitrators if you will—providing us a basis for law with the Ten Commandments. In many respects these "rules and regulations," were the foundation upon which our Founding Fathers, with their Judeo-Christian influence, wanted to strike a balance.

A balance made by respecting all religions, yet keeping them separate from the affairs of the state. Still, we pledge allegiance to one nation under God, have $20 bill declare boldly on the back, "In God We Trust" over the White House. On the back of a 100 (I'm talking about the one with Benjamin), the same words—this time over Independence Hall. Separating us, to the consternation of much of the world, our presidents often proclaim after their speeches "God Bless America," and quite possibly—with the great gift of the Jews—quite possibly, she has…

Today is the 31st of May 2003. It is the Shabbat, and at exactly 08:30 I began to write. The streets are relatively quiet; there is a relaxed calm. So many of my fellow Angelenos, fellow Americans, fellow world travelers, have altered their weekly routines to catch up on rest and sleep in or sleep off or maybe even sleep over.

A life of prepositions, we try to find our place in the world.

Around we go, next to nothingness under pressure, overextended, inside out, beyond reach, behind the concept, in deep shit, out of control; and some of these locations are literal and others figurative. But figuring it all out is literally half the battle; knowing who you are and your position in life—king or pawn, rook or knight, bishop or

William Bradford Borden

queen—is half the game; adapting and modifying, bending and breaking—the rules—is the other.

Would you like half-and-half with your coffee? And as the raging bull steam-rolled toward the objective the crowd screamed "Olay," as the blood of life—the matador's that is—shot profusely onto the bull, over the bull and into the bull, as man and beast became one, sacrificing for one another in a game of life. A bunch of bullshit, you might think, but I guess that depends on how you play the game. And if, for that matter, you're really a player at all, as you sit in the stands in boxes or bleachers and drink your coffee. Aulait! "Shabbat Shalom!"

I write "Shabbat Shalom" a lot and I want to make sure you remember from previous chapters the essence of the word "Shalom," which could mean "hello" or "goodbye." If the Beatles sang in Hebrew their song that examines the paradox of goodbyes and hellos, wouldn't it sound pretty cool? Instead of the conflict created by "hello and goodbye," instead it could be, "You say Shalom and I say Shalom. Shalom, Shalom... I don't know why you say Shalom, I say Shalom."

Anyway, "Shabbat" means Saturday, the Sabbath, "sabado," and in fact the true seventh day, and therefore the true day of rest. Rest in peace, right? Let's hope; and that is the third meaning of Shalom: "peace." And on this last day of May, the day after the real Memorial Day, I ask you, "Do we ever give peace a chance?"

Perhaps to us—especially Americans and our Israeli brothers and sisters, as well—the concept of peace is captivating, but for many of us this is the essence of the predicament; we don't want to be held captive. We don't want to be domesticated, we don't want to play by the rules; no, in fact many of us like a good fight. We like seeing the bull win once in a while, and we like to hunt. It is in our nature.

So one of the most daring games we play, where the rules and engagement are often murky, is the game of war—hunters and hunted, fighting each other, fighting ourselves, fighting domestication. And it seems impossible to imagine, giving peace a chance, as you drive by in your Beatle, past the Dakota and toward ground zero, listening to how stern everyone's become, feeling sluggish rather than bullish, but the Yankees are playing tonight and

American Perversity
Sex, Politics and Religion

ain't nobody gonna' drop a bomb on the Bronx. Yeah, Baby, take me out to the ball game...

If games have rules—and I would imagine that, by definition, a game would almost have to have rules—then one might suggest, and so I will, that the "rules," the foundation, as I alluded to before—of our Judeo-Christian laws are the Ten Commandments. How fitting: 10, completion, perfection, a baseball team and a coach, a minion. What are the 10, from the prescriptive tablets, set in stone? I'll get you the complete list later...

It is late evening now, and I have had a long break. Earlier in the day I sold my Porsche 928 to a Marine major, who appreciated the soul and the power of the car. This is a terrible transition, but I had to lay something down and so I decided on that; but, I must say I have always been surprised by how many Jewish friends drive fancy German cars.

I don't think this chapter will delve into the Holocaust, because this chapter is supposed to be a tribute and celebration of America and the Jews, and so I will not negate the discussion, but leave it for another time and another place. But I will say that in my opinion, that the cause of the Holocaust had a lot more to do with envy than religion, and that is where I am now, in the middle of America, at the "R," yes in America, Religions 'R' U.S.

Yes we pledge allegiance, wave our flags and pay the bills as we deficit spend with our trust funds. How do we justify this? Do we really feel separated in our church and state? Do we really believe? "In God We Trust..." and if all else fails, if you have an "axis" to grind, then perhaps, to let the world know that we're a cut above the rest, we can proclaim—or rather—bow our heads solemnly and pray, "God bless America."

Certainly, our founding fathers were highly influenced by Judeo-Christian principles, the rule of law, and the Ten Commandments:

I.   "I am the Lord your God who has taken you out of the land of Egypt, from the house of slavery."
II. "You shall have no other gods but me."
III. "You shall not take the name of your Lord in vain."
IV. "You shall remember and keep the Sabbath day holy."

155

William Bradford Borden

V. "Honor your father and mother."

VI. "You shall not kill."

VII.   "You shall not commit adultery."

VIII.   "You shall not steal."

IX. "You shall not bear false witness against your neighbor."

X. "You shall not covet your neighbor's goods. You shall not covet your neighbor's house. You shall not covet your neighbor's wife, or his manservant, or his maidservant, or his bull, or his donkey, or anything that is your neighbor's."

Well, there they are, and look—number 10 doesn't say anything about Porsches or Mercedes...

Anyway, enough of all these rules and regulations; it's time to see some of the rest of AMERICA, and so I move to Advertising and Art. Because there is a huge link, between advertising and art—which we will see in the entertainment section—in regards to film, television and print, it would therefore make sense that there is also a substantial influence in advertising with the Jews—think Madison Avenue, and placing the products.

Like I stated earlier, this chapter will be more of a who's who, and so, with the terrific source of www.yahoodi.com—"Famous Jews Interactive"—I give you in the realm of Art: Frida Kahlo, "Mexican artist famous for vivid, surrealist self-portraits"; Leonardo Da Vinci, (for him they say there is "evidence" he was a Jew); Marc Chagall, "Painter, designer and graphic artist, 1887-1985"; Camille Pissarro, "Father of Impressionism, 1830-1903; Frank Gehry, "Pre-eminent architect, designer of Guggenheim Bilbao" and now the Walt Disney Concert Hall; Peter Max "Painter, his designs defined the sixties."

Moving on to medicine...

Before I move on to medicine, I need to refer to the Brokaw chapter, where in essence I said that the evening news was sponsored by drug cartels, and these drugs have connections. There are connections with the prescription drug dealers and the Madison Avenue advertising firms that help these dealers push their products.

Wouldn't it be great if Clinton could take Dole's place as the spokesman for Viagra? What would the spot look like? Maybe, it could open with Clinton at a dry cleaner's picking up a dress in Santa

156

American Perversity
Sex, Politics and Religion

Monica, and he could say, "What it is?" to a wise, black sax player blowing his horn outside. And the weathered, ebony-colored man could slyly say to Bill, "That depends on your definition of 'is'" and Bill could blush, and reach for the sax and say, "Let me blow your horn." (And the black man would say, "Nobody blows my horn," and Bill would say) I separate out that parenthetical part because jokes are supposed to go in three. So, instead, the black man could hold the dress, Bill could blow and a voice-over—perhaps the voice of Hillary—could say, "What's different about Bill? He's found Viagra. Now he can't keep his horn in his case..."

I wonder if anyone would produce such a commercial—perhaps on *Saturday Night Live*. I imagine it would be fun to write copy and try to get people to buy products that they don't need, don't really want and can't really afford. That is probably not the strongest case of connection with conspiracy, but the connection between drugs and advertising does seem more compelling to me than much of America's fiscal, environmental and "defense" policy.

The very word "advertising" is an interesting one to me in that it has 11 letters, and the middle, the "t", almost seems like a cross that connects the first half "adver" with the second half "I sing," and isn't that what advertisers want you to do? Sing their jingles, hum dumbly along, and then, when you feel the urge to consume—conspicuously perhaps—you probably aren't even remotely aware of all the subliminal messages that have been etched into your psyche.

How amazing. I just called (800) 325-3535, and the message said, "Thank you for calling Sheraton..."—Wow! That commercial was more than 20 years old, perhaps 30, and I still remember the jingle "8-0-0 3-2-5 3-5-3-5 "—astounding, but so effective.

Remember the McDonald's campaign for Big Macs—two whole beef patties, special sauce, cheese, pickles, lettuce on a sesame seed bun (I think that's right)? Or, "Where's the Beef?" or how about recent campaigns like "Just Do It," "Got Milk?" or if you don't like milk, I bet you'd "Like to teach the world to sing, in perfect harmony..."

Maybe Madison Avenue would like to see more people sing perfect advertising. But nothing is perfect and there is an art in manipulating the masses. It certainly does help the economy.

William Bradford Borden

Yes, buying and selling are great for the economy and for the creators; but the masses, the "re-creators," are often left with empty pockets, empty minds and empty souls...

...As they fill up with junk, breathe in the banal, and drink at the fountain of false promises as America is franchised away and the individual is treated like an idiot as the CEOs shake your hand smiling, but really laughing at you...

... As they get into their German cars, drink their French wine and vacation in the Virgin Islands, where they've established offshore corporations to avoid paying taxes, and yet their voices are heard much more than yours.

We think, or are led to believe, that it's the "economy stupid"—no, that is not quite correct—it is the stupid economy.

On the 31st of May 2003, in North Carolina, home of Billy Graham and the heart of the Bible belt, police captured the alleged Olympic Park and abortion clinic bomber, Eric Rudolph. There are lots of sympathizers and some people seem to be supporting his actions. What is most troubling to me is when I read that he was one of these renegades that held deep anti-Semitic views because of his belief in their "control" of so much.

Like the Germans, he lost control—not, I imagine, so much out of religious views (now so many of the Southern conservative coalition are lining up behind Israel) but because of sheer envy. He will have lots of time in prison to be even more envious when he realizes he doesn't quite measure up, and that his pen is even weaker than his sword.

For what it's worth, I think he should be imprisoned—if he is guilty—for the rest of his life. Surely, today's capital punishment is too humane and people like Timothy McVeigh get the easy way out while actually costing the taxpayers more money in legal appeals.

There is often a perception of the Jews being physically weak, but having grown up with these people, done a military operation in Israel and lived with an Israeli goddess—Revital, a true "sexy beast"—I can assure you that nothing could be further from the truth. Certainly their numbers are low, but their resolve, their might and their fight is virtually unparalleled.

American Perversity
Sex, Politics and Religion

As much of the Middle-East world knows, you do not want to tangle with the descendents of Abraham, Isaac and Jacob, for many will die, as the most formidable force—man for man, woman for woman—that ever lived will wail from Jerusalem, scream from Tel Aviv and cry out from Masada. "Never again, never again, never again..."

Have you ever done something and then said "never again"? Do you believe that when you are down you should medicate? How do you get through those days of despair? Again, I revert to questions and to a self-Socratic dialogue, peeling away the layers and trying to get to the core, and we would say, as we marched, "One, two, three four, United States Marine Corps," and again I think of getting to the essence, to the center, to the heart of what really matters.

I sit outside by the fountain at the Encino Starbucks and, as I mentioned earlier, the crowd here, seven or so miles from Studio City, is overwhelmingly Middle Eastern, predominately Persian, and I would imagine a solid mix of Muslim and Jew.

A former student of mine, Josef, a Persian Jew, just sat down with me for a half hour and we played a couple games of backgammon, a Middle Eastern game. It was enjoyable to let my mind go, no need of alcohol or drugs, just thought and talk, and movement of pieces, rolls of dice, and pleasant victory. It is an honor to be in the presence of these people and to be in the present and to be thankful for the moment, and the moments do tick by, in L.A. and America, in Tehran and Iran, ticking by like the beats of our hearts until, one day—and some believe it is written—the tick-tock stops and everything is tallied up and that is life.

Not surprisingly, much of the world doesn't currently have a very favorable view of us in America. In the news recently I read that only 38 percent of the people in Spain thought favorably of us. In Germany and France, both less than 50 percent of the people felt favorably toward us. And many Americans may think, "who cares?" and I must say, "I certainly do."

I think all of us should. I really do believe that it would be nice to give peace a chance and try to work a little harder to bridge the gaps and try to understand and get to know each other better.

William Bradford Borden

I think if we did that we could really find paradise, find the truth and the answers to so many of the questions that have relatively straightforward answers. But instead, we seem to always be looking backward and not even comprehending that the greatest weapon of mass destruction is ignorance, and in this age of information it seems so unfortunate that we have been blessed by such possibility and opportunity, but because of our blinders we don't even see. If then, we don't see, maybe it's even harder to hear...

Finding the focus; indeed, that must be one of the themes of this book with a solid mix of sex, politics and religion. So, the focus now is on Jews in medicine, the "M" in AMERICA, and I think that America would make such a lovely name for a daughter, and do people even think of names when they give them, or for that matter know their very meaning, or do most of us go through life with a title for which we have no clue as to what it represents?

Right now a blonde waits in line with "Bilabong" on her back. I am wearing a green sweatshirt with "USMC" over the heart over the eagle, globe and anchor, and soon I will start a couple of clothing lines. One for surfers and snow boarders called *Starsux*—see www.starsux.com, and another for women who know the power of their sex called *Prinsex*—see www.prinsex.com. And you will remember that the "C" in AMERICA represents Clothing.

But, I ask again, who and what do you represent? For which labels, letters and logos do you pay extra money so you can represent their line? And again, I am appalled by how many people are wearing this one line, a line that makes it look like you actually made the team, when in reality most of the wearers send a message to me that they are spectators, elite box holders, perhaps, who belong in the bleachers.

The "M" in AMERICA could also stand for mother and the proverbial Jewish mother, and now some mother enters in with a pink, faded shirt. She wears the number "55" on the front, in white, underneath "Hamptons"—as if she actually played something for the Hamptons—as if, for that matter, she's ever even been to the Hamptons.

Over my shoulder, outside at the green table where I often sit, there is a young guy with a baseball-type t-shirt. White with blue

American Perversity
Sex, Politics and Religion

sleeves reach down to his forearms, and on the front, there are blue letters, over the white, also faded, looking like the shirts that real players, participators, varsity letter winners used to earn. That look that came from sweat and washings—or lack of washings—but now, the game is at the mall; anyone can play. And his "team" is sponsored by so-and-so with the long ass last name and his partner with a short one. Ain't that a bitch? Do you want to throw a fit? You've actually got to pay to play. He thinks he's a player. His number is 22—but, it really isn't his. No, they've got that.

Moms have also got their children's numbers and it seems that the proverbial Jewish mom even more so than most. Talk about moms and medicine, where would we be without chicken soup? But even more healing from moms, I would suggest, comes from their love, encouragement and protection.

I have heard and read so often how so many of our diseases, our illnesses, our maladies, are psychosomatic—of the mind. Creative fiction, and in this self-mind fuck we seem to crate chaos, stress and unnecessary hardship. What is your vehicle of relief, your stress reducer? Is your body truly a temple or do you treat it like a whore in a crack house, or a crack head in a whorehouse, and do you value your health and heal?

Day in and day out... And think once again of David Bloom who died of some kind of blood clot, and the flow of life was damned, but not his life, which he lived to the fullest, day in and day out, knowing that truly—like the Dalai Lama suggested—truly the key to happiness was in giving love, not worrying about receiving love. And surely we would be much happier if we gave more that we received, and yet the Christian "Lord's Prayer" pleads, "Give us this day" and I ask, "What do we do with the day once it's been given?"

I hope this is starting to add up. According to www.qchillel.org, 30 percent of Nobel Prize winners in medicine are Jews. To me, these numbers are astounding because according to the same site, the number of Jews in the world's population is 0.3 percent; phenomenal, and I would assert that the numbers truly speak for themselves.

Back to the yahoodi.com site, just a few of the famous Jews in medicine: Jonas Salk (developed the first polio vaccine); Nostradamus (1503-1566, Jewish Doctor and Prophet) and Paul

William Bradford Borden

Ehrlich (Nobel Prize for discovering a treatment for syphilis) and the list could go on and on, but it's starting to give me a headache, so I think I'll get some entertainment—it's time for a break...

On to some entertainment, the "E" of AMERICA, which I will combine with "I" for Industry because entertainment is an industry and that would be the most industrious move, and if I don't try to clothe my motives in shrouds of deceit, I just might get the "C" in as well—and so we move toward the completion and the fullness of Chapter 10, of AMERICA, of the Jews...

In today's West Coast edition of the *New York Times*, a week or so before Father's Day, on page three, in the bottom right corner, a handsome, smiling model, shirt open, and it reads Kenneth Cole, and underneath that, in larger font, all caps, GIFTS DAD LOVES.

Certainly clothing is big business and when you look at the power and influence of such companies as Calvin Klein, Ralph Lauren, Kenneth Cole, Guess?, and Levi Strauss, one can once again appreciate the power and influence of the Jews.

But there is also something that the envious, anti-Semites are missing. What they are missing is the creativity and craft of the Jews, and so now, for a list of some of the chosen.

I am diverted, as a "chosen" group outside, five men, talk about... divorce, child support, negotiations, some attorneys, and the talk is loud, inflammatory and elevated, "keeping ex out of the loop. "Fuck, you didn't go to the bank and get anything out? My ex took 20 thousand in the last week. Make her pay fucking half," (on and on they go, a crescendo of poetry, some rapt verse, improvisational...) "I'm telling you the system sucks...days I sat there...you make all the money...your wife has a kid on each tit—that used to be my spot. Twenty thousand gone in a week...the judge doesn't realize you're not even getting your dick sucked...why should we have to support them for the rest of their lives?"

On and on they banter. The institution of marriage is obviously broken. And now the loud, vocal one, a short angry man, starts again but Eric Estrada, the famous actor who played the motorcycle cop on CHiPS walks by to go in for a coffee. He is handsome, black suit, open blue shirt, his hair full, with a nice mix of salt and pepper, and one of the guys asks Eric—and he is kind and open and cool—how

162

American Perversity
Sex, Politics and Religion

many Rolls Royces he has, and Estrada says, "Two, a white one and a black one." Right before he enters the Starbucks, he smiles and says, "My ex took the rest."

I want to give this argument a rest, but when I see what my dear friend, who is like a sister to me, has gone through with her divorce and her "Mac-daddy" husband's deceit, lies and evasion in regard to his liaisons with escorts, his hiding of financial documents, and his general disregard for honesty—it makes me, in combination with this conversation to my right, want to swear off marriage and all its problems, but I still would love to be a father. Now Erick Estrada is back out, and one of the five, the half minion, tells Erick that some woman wants him, but he says he's married now and has three kids, and he is calm, cool and collected, and he says he doesn't do that shit anymore as he walks south, to his Rolls...

Adam Sandler, who is Jewish, has a terrific Hanukah song where he lists famous Jews in entertainment, and so we move to the "E" of AMERICA. For my source, I will use the www.yahoodi.com site, the one previously mentioned under the title "Famous Jews Interactive," and because this is the 10th chapter, and 10 is the number of completeness, the number of the minion, I have chosen 10 from each category of the page long lists. Any parenthetical reference will be Yahoodi's.

In the field of acting the following are Jewish: Winona Ryder, Cary Grant, Gwyneth Paltrow, William Shatner, Sarah Jessica Parker, Paul Newman, Michael Douglas, Dustin Hoffman, Daniel Day-Lewis, and Goldie Hawn.

In the field of directing and producing, the Jewish nominees are: Steven Spielberg, Stanley Kubrick, Mel Brooks, Sam Mendes, Neil Simon, Woody Allen, Roman Polanski, Oliver Stone, Billy Wilder and Aaron Spelling.

In the field of music and singing: Barry Manilow, Al Jolson, Bob Dylan, Billy Joel, Barbara Streisand, Elvis Presley ("The King of Rock and Roll—yes, the king has unbroken Jewish roots."), Neil Diamond, Bette Midler, Lou Reed, and Paul Simon and Art Garfunkel.

Earlier, I mentioned that more than 30 percent of the Nobel Prize winners in medicine were Jewish and so I have also chosen 10 Nobel

William Bradford Borden

Prize winners, not all in the scientific realm, to show the remarkable achievement of such a small number. These 10, I will include the parenthetical references from Yahoodi.com's excellent site.

The winners are: Albert Einstein (the most famous and influential scientist of all time): Richard Feynman (the greatest scientific mind since World War II); Rita Levi-Montalcini (winner of the Nobel Prize for her work on nerve growth); Elie Wiesel (author, winner of Nobel Prize for peace); Isaac Bashevis Singer (author, Nobel Prize winner for literature); Milton Friedman (recipient of the Nobel Memorial Prize in economics); Paul Samuelson (Nobel Prize in Economics—first ever); Franco Modigliani (Italian-born economist, 1985 Nobel Prize Laureate in Economics) and Saul Bellow (Nobel Prize winner for Literature).

Because the Jews have been called the "People of the Book," and their book, the Old Testament, has certainly set the foundation for modern Western and American society, and because books are, in my opinion, some of the greatest gifts one can give—and because the Jews have given us this gift, the gift of words, of stories, of books—I find it only fitting that I end this chapter and this book with authors.

The authors I have chosen are—and, unfortunately, the first was chosen, for another reason, and for that reason we must never forget, Anne Frank, Isaac Asimov, Arthur Miller, Judy Blume, Ayn Rand, Carl Sagan, Danielle Steele, Chaim Potok, and Gertrude Stein.

Five men, five women, finding balance, complementing one another, complementing a people, and, although not all American, they represent AMERICA and I have chosen them because, quite possibly, they were chosen long before.

And as the great minions assemble across America—this Friday, this evening, this Shabbat, to give thanks and pray, to study and argue—let us hope that we can all learn something about doing what is right, what is true, and what is good. Let us do it with love...for it is written. Shabbat Shalom.

Epilogue

Nine years and one month after my father left this earth—and I was going to write "died," and then thought "passed away" but decided on "left this earth;" and yet that doesn't really work because he is somehow still here and always will be—nine years and one month after my father, the former vice president of in-flight service for TWA went on a timeless journey, a first class trip, a permanent vacation, I wrote him this letter and sent it air mail, through the cosmos of space and time—somehow, I'm sure he got it...

Dear Dad,   13 Dec. 99 Encino, CA

As I begin to write this letter I realize I don't know where the pen shall guide me or rather where I shall guide the pen. "Words, words, words," said Shakespeare. Yes, these are words. You knew I loved Shakespeare. In fact the summer before you died I went to Stratford and studied Shakespeare.

When I was in Stratford I fell in love with Christy and she is now on a major soap opera. That was nine years ago. She is on a soap opera and my life is one. I remember being back in NJ and I had just bought a video recorder and I was taping people. You said I was so good interviewing people. I asked what you thought of me and you said that I had many gifts but often wasted them.

William Bradford Borden

Somehow, when I went to Stratford, I copied over that tape. That same summer, right when I came back from England, Barbara's baby Rebecca was born and I was alerted that there were problems—that was so hard for everyone but you were there and I worshipped you as I always had.

At the same time the Gulf War heated up and although my stint in the Marine Corps was up, I was in the reserves and on stand-by. Times were tense. And then that great Marine Corps birthday—you know how much I used to look at your pictures of you as an 18 year old corpsman on Bougainville and Guadalcanal— on the Marine Corps Birthday, Nov. 10, 1990, you had a heart attack. I was in graduate school in North Carolina, and ironically with a male friend Asle from Norway playing the piano.

I have never had many male friends because I had you and you were my god, my hero and my father. What more did I need? I caught up with Mom at the airport. She was flying in from San Diego after visiting Barbara and the baby who wasn't created equal.

Yesterday I wrote Mom a letter and I shared it with her today. You would have been proud of me. I think she feels that I always cared more for you than her. Maybe I did. Maybe though some of the reasons I caused such wrath and destruction was not only that I wanted your attention, but maybe it was also Oedipal in nature.

Maybe I wanted what you had. When you died on Nov. 13, 1990, 3 days after the Marine Corps birthday, part of me died. The part that wanted to share, experience and sacrifice for love. Just over a month ago on Nov. 13, 1999, Mom, Barbara and Brian, along with Uncle Lee went out to your parent's grave site in Marysville and Mom brought your ashes (some of them from NJ). We all said something one by one.

166

American Perversity
Sex, Politics and Religion

It really was a moving experience and seeing the name William Ross next to your Mom and acknowledging that you were William Stephenson and I am William Bradford and all the other William Bordens in our line was powerful.

What was more powerful was what Mom said and that was that you died too soon and that you were so loving and that what made your relationship work was that you never went to sleep without resolving and issue.

I need to resolve issues. Nine years after your death, on that anniversary (it was also the 50th wedding anniversary of your sister Becky) I resolved them and had a sense of completion. Still, this letter lets me fully realize the impact of all these experiences.

I realize now that in some respects you were just as married to TWA, and that the airline was just as much a part of your family as we were. The tape I copied over was gone, but there are the segments from *60 Minutes and Nightline* which were on tape. So what. It is what it is.

Mom gets upset with me when I rant against corporate America because she believes this provided me with the opportunities and comforts I have. Yes, it left her very wealthy, but it also left you dead at 65 and I regret that. Notice I didn't say resent. I regret not being able to hear your laughter, to hug you, to squeeze your biceps, to smell you, to look you in the eye, to talk to you. But now I am talking to you. It is spiritual. Tears are streaming down my face and somehow I'm being healed.

On your deathbed you really wanted me to teach and to do a PhD. You so enjoyed teaching at Rutgers. I remember you saying or asking if I was a good teacher and I said, "Not bad." I asked you the same thing; it was the day before you died, and you looked

167

William Bradford Borden

me in the eye, weakly smiled and said, "Not bad, not bad."

Thank you for the gift of life and teaching me to love. Maybe you didn't teach it to me because I've never forgotten it and you only forget that which you can learn. I am trying Dad.

Anyway, God I'm sobbing, but you know that don't you, I'm opening up new possibilities in my life and the possibility that I am inventing for myself and the possibility that I am inventing for myself and my life is the possibility of being someone who has the wonderful and powerful joy of freedom, love and laughter with the responsibility of creative and musical expression in the process of being spiritual and reaching Nirvana.

Love from your son,
William Bradford and Borden

Acknowledgements

With the Most Sincere
Appreciation, Gratitude and Respect

My brother **Brian** for his friendship,

My sister **Barbara** for her example, virtue and tenacity,

My life-long friends **Doug**, **Jay**, and **Sharon**,

Share Bear for her light, hope, and joy.

Tonie Lee Perensky for her encouragement, friendship and advice,

Alison Heimburger for her amazing editing, attitude and attention to detail,

Sir Ed Lawrence for his guidance, direction and wisdom,

Joy "Joyfully" for her assistance, presence, and positive attitude,

Shirley Pakdaman for her gift, her words, and her kindness,

Jennifer StGermain for her thoughtfulness, joy and wisdom,

Michelle "Mikey" Cherry for her confidence, assistance and support,

William Bradford Borden

Megan, Shirley, and Tania "Kamala" for their typing,

Bernie Daly for his suggestion of *Far From Mary*,

My teachers, for their nurturing:
Mrs. Hauck, Miss Jones, Mrs. DeMatias, Mrs. Kontakis, Mrs. McDowell, Mrs. Fields, Mrs. Young, Mr. Terrell, Mr. Job, Mr. Foster, Ms. Lookstein, Ms. Stahl, Mr. Fausty,

My professors, for their experience:
Dr. Amante, Dr. Jacoby, Dr. Davis, Dr. Hemley, Dr. Smith, Dr. Patton, Dr. Weiser,

My mentors, for their guidance:
Marina Koshetz, Bobbie Chance-Shaw, Miss Stevenson, Ms. Hayes, Mark Knowles, Brenda Sopher, Donna Accardo, Paul Whalen, Alberto Ferro, Sergio Chirotti, Ilza Prestinari, Elizabetta Pession, Ron Sullivan.

My Shakespeareans, for their wisdom:
Phyllis, Janice, Jeannie, Norma, Norman, Fern, Roslyn, Marissa, Stephanie, Marion Sally, Virginia, Susan, David, Hilda, Bernice Rachel, Bernice, Malcolm, Louise, Ludwig, Nancy, Joseph, Shirley, Bill, Patricia, Carol, Yvonne, Ed, Carolee, Sallee, Martin, George, Blanche, Mary, Lowell, Erroll, Marie, John, Maria, Charlene, Bonnie, Violet, Larry, Jerry,

My students, for their goodness:
Christopher, Ali, Shayna, Janet, Erica, Molly, Neiri, Matthew, Jessica, Jennifer, Marques,
Dava, Branko, Brian, Pamela, Shelly, Danielle, Shyann

Tony, David, Justin, Duriel, Max, Luiza, Ryan, Natalie, Louverne, Elina, Joey, Mary, Ely, Marjoie, Jeremy, Roman, Manuel, Jorge

American Perversity
Sex, Politics and Religion

Bizhan, Gil, David, Jonathan, Krystal, Jessic, Freda, Jaime, Erica, Joung Hee, Daniel, Shaw, Scott, Yajaira, Stella, Angelica, Gladys, Kristine, Ariel, Cindy, Aura, Domarina, Alexandra, Ryan, Jamie, Jennifer, Amela, Toon, Poy Hing, Trevor

Manuk, Kareemah, Josh, Ismael, Jacqueline, Sarai, Josh, Darrell, Gemma, Laura, Guillermo, Jessica, Crystal, Donna, Jessica, Hanzel, Clarissa, Douglas, Nancy.
Mayra, Keanna, Edgar, Melissa, Spencer, Raquel, Michael

Wesley, Karla, Jason, Tyler, Temma, David, Daniel, Andrea, Freddy, Byron, Michelle, Albert, Hylda, Kit, Ronald

Rebecca, Jordan, David, Paul, Emily, Ram, Eric, Ryan, John, Hilary, Michelle, Brenda, Robert, Ryan, Margaret, Allan, Michael Eric, Michael, Greg, Mark, Maayan, Walter, Azniv, Felipe, Vivian, Whitney

Billy, Farrah, Sabrina, Jasen, Jessica, Nazely, Tyler, Josh, Knar, Keren, Daniel, Natalie, Antonio, Jorge, Marlon, Noah, Carlos, Oscar

Prabhjot, Sherman, Gennifer, Claudia, Dontra, Sarita, David, Tanya, Shaun, Krishna, Tiffany, Blanca, Binh, Brenda, Leah, Greg, Freddy, Francisco,

Ousanna, Eloisa, Maura, Adrean, Michael, Marcos, Conor, Donna, Parham, Isabella, Shoshana, Raul, Natalie, Olimpia, Samantha

Claudia, Alexis, Sarah, Arnaz, Cindy, Carlos, Blanca, Gevork, Georde, Dorly, Patricia, Serina,

Victor, Nabat, Michelle, Amandeep, Brisley, Robyn, Claudiu, Jose, Sara, Corina, Courtney, Jennifer, Angel, Seth, Christopher, James, Gerald, Shirley, Maria, Leiannon, Michael, Chinere, Deborah, Sandra, Timothy, Erik, Liya, Mary, Arash, Ben, Sheila, Shauna, Scott, Greg

William Bradford Borden

Eveline, Diego, Lisa, Alma, Megan, Tracy, Jakob, Rachel, Erica, Deanna, Anthony, Igor, Nikki, Michael, Pablo, Andriana, Saman, Geo, Maurice, Jennifer, Justin, Maria, Erica, Karen, Diana, Maytal, Ed, Christine, Ronald

Erez, Cyrus, Marie, Victoria, Nadia, Nikkolene, Debra, Vania, Walter, Sharona, Matthew, Joe, Michaela, Sharey, Won Ho, Daniel, Ron, Jessica, Melissa, Orna, Mitchell, Jennifer, Kia, Emeline, Karin, Jung, Michael, Ruby, Khijaan, Angela, Ozra, Bahmen, Kia

Laurel, Michelle, Karla, Thomas, Frankie, Gregoria, John, Rochelle, Bonnie, Tanya, Ryan, Michael, Milena, Princess, Heather, Elena, Robert, Sahar, Walter, Tanaz, Cuong, Reyna, Paul, Erica, Cynthia, Jill, Suzzane,

Mikey, Magdolna, Alma, Hazel, Jaclyn, Kathleen, Jakob, Rachel, Tiffany, Milian, Sepideh, Brian, Christine, Armen, Marissa, Yvette, Karla, Jonathan, Pouneh, Mike, Miriam, Maytal, Maryam, Tiara, Nima, Jennifer, Mohammed, Tara, Maya, Justin, Devon, Karen, Nick

Alma, Karla, Edith, Marisa, Frankie, Sindy, Denise, Tiffany, Bonnie, Sharona, Philip, Beth, Ron, Princess, Mishelle, Pourya, Heather, Jennifer, Nani, Homan, Maria, Walter, Kari, Daniel, Diana, Melody, Lauren, Yelmi, Monica, Diana, Michael, Penny, Ryan, Hector

Quinn, Stephanie, Nazim, Faiza, Michael, Ahmed, Laura, Sara, Arthur, Miguel, Ron, Natalie, Roberto, Josh, Sabrina, Gaudelia, Scott, Jose, Nima, Iman, Radney, Michelle, Muriel, Ava, Leora, Jennifer the Saint

Virginia, Christina, Kelly, Paul, Jodi, Jennifer, Apryl, Debra, Ghazaleh, Lillian, Harmony, Shaun, Claudene, Tanaz, Jorge, Christina, Erin, Sahar, Shannon, Tennelle, Mahta, Anh, Melissa, Hannah, Shirley, Milena, Jung, Michael, Jeremiah, Mindie, Kathy, Navid, Sanaz, Dulanjali, Dorita

American Perversity
Sex, Politics and Religion

Nayri, Kimbery, Brian, Danielle, Lenny, Michael, Aaron, Nazahin, Jane, Michelle, Vahe, Ghazaleh, Mouiz, Joanne, Yomelia, Roben, Rey, Jason, Faraz, Christopher, Norberto, Andrew, Olga, Gareen, Zeenat, Hong, Veneet, Tiffany, Milton, Yelmi, Vincent, Brooke, Geofery, Gabby, Karin

Natalie, Edward, Farnaz, Katherine, Houman, Niloufar, Geraldine, Melanie, Gali, Shirley, Yomelia, Andrew, Olga, Sharon, William, JJ, Rachel, Erica, Vincent, Iman, Sadia, Neda, Eric, Carmen, Radney, Jessica, Katy, Brooke, Gelareh, Babak, Nima

Iam, Atena, Shaghayeh, Paul, Saeah, Areerat, Sankia, Eric, Nancy, Tali, Karen, Deborah, Nicholas, Razmik, Sandra, Daniel, Donna, Elysha, Bonnie, Linda, Tracy, Mayra, Jose, Patrick, Kimberly, Danna, Derek, Ranel, Ronnie, Carly, Irma, Kristy, Shani, Jennifer

Jerry, Megan, Faiza, Lisa, Lenny, Danielle, Canaan, Alice, David, Argyris, Sara, Jennifer, Michelle, Eugene, Ron, Alfred, Jesus, Jose, Veneet, Yanir, Courtney, Alfredo, Erica, Narbeh, Jen, Brice, Charon, Stephanie, Tania, Shlomi, Akbar, Natalie, Cole, Linda, Ghazeleh, Marcus, Caitlin, Stephanie

Aida, Vic, Sonia, Esmeralda, Danial, Houman, Aaron, Jane, Robert, Parham, Marissa, Suhyung, Allison, Juan, Suniel, Seon, Young, Ratna, Alyson, Kenny, Nina, Arash, Larry, Erik, Kristen, Rocio, Nareen, Shmuel, Narinder, Ana, Ericka,

Kelsey, Jennifer, Nima, Obaid, Atena, Tamara, Veronica, Andrea, Jacob, Neda, Tarun, Sara, Devin, Allen, Gerard, Leticia, Jason, Karla, David, Avi, David, Jonathan, Peymen, Alejandra, Tye, Mary, Chloe, Sandra, Jacqueline, Saman, Jonathan, Sophia, Mellanie, Gloria, Joanna, John,

Guillame, Torfeh, Shekar, Padra, Ronit, Matthew, Melody, Jose, Atsushi, Sayeh, Natalie, Eli, Jin, Vanessa, Jarrod, Joanna, Cindy, Reza, Mikhel, William, Jerry, Joshua, Alondra, Janet, Mikyung,

William Bradford Borden

ThuyHa, Pawntia, David, David, Juliana, Susan, Joseph, Nazila, Oren, Natalie, Rodika, Daniela, Ronit

Iam, Rachel, Paul, Juan, Saeah, Jose, Lauren, Irma, Arthur, Maral, Arthur, Maral, Robert, Paul, Juan, Saeah, Jose, Lauren, Irma, Arthur, Maral, Robert, Hasmik, Veronica, Jonathan, Eric, Derek, Rey, Kimberly, Glenda, Nicole, Nick, Nicholas, Kimberly, Ashley, Sandra, Cynthia, Mitchell, Maira, Justin, Karla, Linda, Chaney, Brittany, Ranel, Lilly, Lara, Shaghayeh, Shabazz

Liliana, Gladys, Michael, Jannina, Guillermo, Jill, Jennifer, Elan, Lilia, Nitin, Jose, Nicholas, Julia, Silvia, Brent, Daniel, Shaun, Sylvia, Mario, Shane

Hovik, Megan, Leili, Robert, Lindsay, Jellyn, Shamis, Natalie, Carmen, Benjamin, Assal, Azadeh, Genna, Sanaz, Angela, Kate, Erin, Tae-Kwang, Shirley, Karlina, Lauren, Fernando, Teena, Justin, Merlin, Olga, Jose, Harmonie, Anita, Fatima, Mike, Rochelle, Xigian

Victor, Fanny, Maricarmen, Ingrid, Isis, Tania, Yaron, Chantal, Cindy, Vasilis, Mariam, Sadayasu, Tamila, Jeffrey, Humaira, Khatera, Daniel, Junichi, Moran, Christine, Linda, Dana Rose, Kathryn, Annie, Brent, Rheza, Leno, Christi, Isidoro, Greg, Laura, Sean, Kristy, Malisa, Mark, Albert, Leslie, Melissa

Julie, Mary Grace. Mario, Joshua, Wei-Min, Sam, David, Darrell, Juliana, Daniel, Sogol, Arezo, Latrisha, Sarah, Elmira, Caroline, Aryan, Alan, Charlene, Amir, Josheph, Naureen, Dao, Romelia, Jeffrey, Shani, Aryan, Mohammad, Kamran, Andrew, Sheena, Farshad, Mani, Jeffrey, Fnu, Omid

Golnoush, Aida, George, Tonirose, Demetriux, Julie, Ayla, Yao-Hsuan, Avivit, Galynne, Shunji, Moran, Tina, Farnaz, Waheeda, AJ, Nicole, Roxanne, Agni, Leno, Colby, Dulce, Emily, Crystal, Nayeli, Isaac, Max, Alexis, Leonel, Shannon, Parisa, Arcineh, Sally, Melanie, Maryam, Christine

About the Author

Bradford Borden is an adjunct English professor in Los Angeles, CA. The recipient of two consecutive Golden Apple Awards, Borden teaches composition, literature and Shakespeare. He also serves on the diversity committee and is the snowboard club advisor. He has a Master of Arts in English from the University of North Carolina at Charlotte, with an emphasis in rhetoric.

Prior to arriving in Los Angeles, he lived in Rome Italy, from 1991-1993, where he acted, wrote and taught English. He starred as an American writer in the Italian film *Una Casa Sotto il Cielo* (*A House under the Sky*). In Italy he also had the opportunity to work with Nick Nolte, F. Murray Abraham and Ben Cross. He is a member of the Screen Actors Guild and attended the American Academy of Dramatic Arts in Hollywood, CA.

Borden is also a graduate of the California Military Academy and spent five years in the U.S. Marine Corps. He earned medals from all branches of the service and participated in military operations and deployments to Japan, Belize, the Phillipines, Korea and Israel.

He currently resides in Los Angeles, California.

Printed in the United States
17700LVS00006B/223-282